Eliza

Keith and Ann Terry

KenningHouse
Orem, Utah

Copyright © 1981, 1995 By Keith & Ann Terry
Published By KenningHouse
1087 East 680 North
Orem, UT 84057
ISBN: 1-57636-002-4

Dedication

To Waynard and Jean Lowe, who encouraged our early efforts.

Acknowledgments

We extend appreciation to JoAnn Jolly and Garth Rasmussen for extensive preliminary research in the historical archives of the L.D.S. Church as well as universities and libraries.

Special thanks for the editorial assistance of Nora Jacob, who is without a doubt one of the finest editors in America. Also, for the able team efforts of Marilyn Griffin, who typed and retyped the manuscript.

Eliza—A Poetess Comes To Zion

Chapter One

The slight woman of 27 leaned forward in her chair at one side of the large open fireplace at her parents' home in Mantua, Ohio, that chilly January evening. Her dark hair, pulled back at the forehead, hung in ringlets about her head, allowing tiny gold earrings to be seen plainly. Eliza Roxcy Snow had never lived away from her family or the comfortable two-story house she loved. It was the finest home in town, rivalling several in the county in 1832.

That evening she felt especially excited. The famed prophet Joseph Smith had dropped in to visit with Eliza's parents. She, as well as they, counted it an honor to have the Mormon prophet sit beside the fire speaking to them while warming his chilled hands.

Eliza studied the Prophet's features, trying to determine if in fact he was a prophet of God or an imposter. For some time Eliza had experienced a yearning to hear a prophet—a prophet like Moses. She and her family had recently attended church services at nearby Hiram, Ohio. They had watched in admiration men such as Sidney Rigdon join the new Mormon faith and immediately lead the congregation with a new spirit about him.

Eliza knew that her family, at least her mother and sister, were ready to be baptized. But she herself needed more time. Eliza considered herself well-read and possibly a notch above those around her when it came to intellectual pursuits. Hers was a quick mind which would rapidly evaluate the merit of a thing. Now she wished to know more about the new sect called Mormonism. Especially did she want to know if Joseph Smith was in very deed a prophet of God.

Very early in her religious experience, Eliza had been moved by those who seemed to be servants of God. Two outstanding religious men had touched her life before she met Joseph Smith: Alexander Campbell and his associate, Sidney Rigdon. Both men had gained followers by the mid-1820s, before the organization of the Church of Jesus Christ of Latter-day Saints. A potent spirit of evangelism had spread along the shores of Lake Erie and deep into the wooded regions of Ohio. At the time of Eliza's first evangelical encounter, she was 16 years old and easily moved. She later wrote, "Feeling that religion was necessary, I sought for it; but, when I asked, like one of old, 'What shall I do to be saved?' and was told that I must have a change of heart, and, to obtain it, I must feel myself to be the worst sinner, and acknowledge the justice of God in consigning me to everlasting torment, the common sense with which God had endowed me, revolted, for I knew I had lived a virtuous and conscientious life, and no consideration could extort from me a confession so absurd. Some told me one thing and some another; but there was no Peter, 'endowed from on high.'"

The closest to a "Peter" that Eliza had heard was the wise Alexander Campbell. That leader's evangelism had swept through Ohio like wildfire.

Campbell, with his father, had founded a sect known as the Disciples of Christ. From 1813 to 1830 the group remained under the nominal aegis of the Baptists. But Campbell stirred up the established Baptists by advocating a return to spiritual simplicity in organization and doctrine. His followers, "Campbellites," became reformers.

Eliza listened. She wrote of that experience, "I heard Alexander Campbell advocate the literal meaning of the Scriptures—listened to him with deep interest—hoped his new life led to a fulness—was baptized, and soon learned that, as well they might, he and his followers disclaimed all authority, and my baptism was of no consequence."

Still, she did not disclaim the group, for she found many benefits to it. Perhaps the most valuable instruction Eliza had garnered from her association with the Campbellites centered on the ancient prophets. She undertook a detailed study of the prophets, learning what to expect should one appear. The erudite Campbell and a Scotsman named Walter Scott tutored her with the assistance of yet a third person, a man whom Eliza would come to know in a lengthier and more complex association— Sidney Rigdon. Rigdon was a friend of the Snow family's, and his influence on them was a profound one.

Oliver and Rosetta Pettibone Snow had first settled in Becket, Massachusetts, where their New England roots had extended deep into an English ancestry. In 1806, two years after the birth of their second child, Eliza, they had moved west to Ohio. There, by the time Sidney Rigdon had become a regular visitor at the Snows' pleasant home in Mantua, five additional children were born, two daughters and three sons.

By occupation a farmer, Eliza's father Oliver also functioned as a civic leader, having early gained the trust of local public officials. By 1829, the Snow family was opening its home to a number of preachers and evangelists traveling through the region. Eliza was constantly exposed to their ideas and sermons. But in the autumn of that year, a new and powerful influence reached the Snows: the *Book of Mormon* came off the press.

Eliza, and undoubtedly her entire family, had known of Joseph Smith since the autumn of 1820, when "six months after young Smith had that astonishing vision of the Father and the Son, the tidings reached my ears that God had spoken from the heavens; that he had raised up a prophet, and was about to restore the fulness of the gospel with all its gifts and powers." Eliza wrote further, "I heard of Joseph Smith as a prophet, to whom the Lord was speaking from the heavens; and that a Sacred Record containing a history of the origin of the aborigines of America, was unearthed."

With Eliza's study of the prophets and her keen interest in history and literature, the notice that a mere mortal was calling himself a prophet must have stirred great curiosity in the young woman. She was preoccupied with the possibility of a coming prophet, an event she later claimed to have awaited for nine years. "A Prophet of God, the voice of God, revealing God's will to man as in former dispensations," Eliza exclaimed in her writings. "It was what my soul had hungered for."

In fact, in 1829, Eliza had written a poem portraying the advent of just such a prophet, and the revelation of truths before unknown:

> But lo! a shining Seraph comes!
>   Hark! 'tis the voice of sacred Truth;
> He smiles, and on his visage blooms,
>   Eternal youth.
>
> He speaks of things before untold,
>   Reveals what men nor angels knew,
> The secret pages now unfold
>   To human view.

The prophetic element of the poem was not overlooked. Years later, after her acceptance of the Mormon gospel, Eliza amended the phrase "secret pages" to read "long seal'd pages," to more fully harmonize her words with the restoration of the gospel by the prophet Joseph Smith.

Always a person critical of hearsay or grandiose claims, Eliza had her doubts. She wondered if the story of Joseph Smith's revelations could "possibly be true—I considered it a hoax—too good to be true."

As the fire dwindled and the embers glowed that January evening, she evaluated this so-called prophet's testimony firsthand.

Joseph Smith had journeyed to Kirtland the previous year to meet there with the growing body of church members, then numbering more than two hundred. At the same time, Sidney Rigdon, the Campbellite, had listened with his followers to the testimonies of missionaries Oliver Cowdery and Parley P. Pratt. As a result, most of the Campbellites in Kirtland had joined the new Mormon religion. After moving to Kirtland permanently later that year, Joseph traveled about the shores of Lake Erie meeting with members and prospective members. In January, 1832, while residing with his wife, Emma, and children at Hiram, Ohio, he rode over to the neighboring community of Mantua to visit the Snow family.

Seated to one side of the room, Eliza kept up her intense study of the Prophet as he spoke. She revealed both her cautiousness and a fascination with the Prophet and his belief in a later sketch of her life written for Howard H. Bancroft in the 1870s:

"He sat warming himself, I scrutinized his face as closely as I could without attracting his attention, and decided that his was an honest face. My adopted motto, 'Prove all things and hold fast that which is good,' prompted me to investigate, as incredulous as I was. . . ." Then she added, "The most impressive testimonies I had ever heard were given by two of the witnesses to the *Book of Mormon*, at the first meeting of the believers in Joseph Smith's mission, which I attended."

It seems likely that Eliza had not only heard about Joseph Smith, but she had attended proselytizing meetings held by Cowdery, Pratt, or one of the other "witnesses" in 1830 when they went through Ohio on their mission to the Lamanites. So the nature of Joseph Smith's testimony, if not the powerful influence of the Prophet's personal delivery, had affected her long before the night they met.

Impressed though Eliza may have been with Joseph Smith, she waited three more years, until 1835, before committing herself to baptism.

Not until Eliza's older sister and her two children returned home to Mantua from Kirtland in early 1835 did Eliza become convinced of the message of the Prophet Joseph. Kirtland was then church headquarters. Her sister told Eliza that she had met the Prophet and stood convinced of the truth of his mission. Eliza immediately took a keener interest in the church and its teachings.

She wrote, "The spirit bore witness to me of the truth. I felt that I had waited already a little too long to see whether the work was going to 'flash in the pan' and go out. But my heart was now fixed." It was April 5, 1835; she was "baptized by a Mormon Elder."

Hers was no ordinary experience. Eliza wanted the power of the Holy Ghost to give direction to her life, and thus her mind and spirit were attuned to receiving that promised gift. On the evening of the April day she was baptized in a stream, Eliza also received the baptism of the Spirit.

"I had retired to bed," she wrote, "and as I was reflecting on the wonderful events transpiring around me, I felt an indescribable, tangible sensation, if I may so call it, commencing at my head and enveloping my person and passing off at my feet, producing inexpressible happiness. Immediately following, I saw a beautiful candle with an unusual long, bright blaze directly over my feet."

Eliza, always alert to symbolic meaning, sought by the spirit of prayer to know the interpretation of her vision. Understanding came to her shortly. The vision of candle and flame above her feet meant, "The lamp of intelligence shall be lighted over your path," Eliza wrote. Lying back on her pillow in the dark of night, she recounted later, "I was satisfied."

One of her earliest poems, entitled "Evening Thoughts or What It Means To Be a Saint," reveals the depth of her convictions:

My heart is fix'd—I know in whom I trust.
'Twas not for wealth—'twas not to gather heaps
Of perishable things—'twas not to twine
Around my brow a transitory wreath,
A garland decked with gems of mortal praise,
That I forsook the home of childhood; that
I left the lap of ease—the halo rife
With friendship's richest, soft, and mellow tones;
Affection's fond caresses, and the cup
O'erflowing with the sweets of social life,
With high refinement's golden pearls enrich'd.

Ah, no! A holier purpose fir'd my soul;
A nobler object prompted my pursuit.
Eternal prospects open'd to my view,
And hope celestial in my bosom glow'd.
God, who commanded Abraham to leave
His native country, and to offer up
On the lone altar, where no eye beheld
But that which never sleeps, an only son,
Is still the same; and thousands who have made
A covenant with him by sacrifice,
Are bearing witness to the sacred truth—
Jehovah speaking has reveal'd his will.

The proclamation sounded in my ear—
It reached my heart—I listen'd to the sound—

Counted the cost, and laid my earthly all
Upon the altar, and with purpose fix'd
Unalterably, while the spirit of
Elijah's God within my bosom reigns,
Embrac'd the everlasting covenant,
And am determined now to be a saint,
And number with the tried and faithful ones,
Whose race is measured with their life; whose prize
Is everlasting, and whose happiness
Is God's approval; and to whom 'tis more
Than meat and drink to do his righteous will.

Although to be a saint requires
A noble sacrifice—an arduous toil—
A persevering aim; the great reward
Awaiting the grand consummation will
Repay the price, however costly; and
The pathway of the saint the safest path
Will prove; though perilous—for 'tis foretold,
All things that can be shaken, God will shake,
Kingdoms and governments, and institutes,
Both civil and religious, must be tried—
Tried to the core, and sounded to the depth.

Then let me be a saint, and be prepar'd
For the approaching day, which like a snare
Will soon surprise the hypocrite—expose
The rottenness of human schemes—shake off
Oppressive fetters—break the gorgeous reins
Usurpers hold, and lay the pride of man—
The pride of nations, low in dust!

A cold December wind tugged the reins in her gloved hands. Eliza was pert and more youthful seeming than five years earlier when she had first encountered the Mormon beliefs. Now, several months after her baptism, the fragile brunette had left Mantua to join her newly adopted people, planning to enmesh her life with those of the Saints at Kirtland. Of that arrival in 1835, Eliza wrote that she was "happy in an association with the saints, fully appreciating their enlarged views and rich intelligence from the fountain of Eternal Truth, through the inspiration of the Most high...."

Her move to Kirtland was fortuitous for Joseph and Emma Smith because they had been searching for a tutor for their young children. They had heard of Eliza's skills in writing, as well as of her training as a teacher. Merely to speak with the educated lady and hear her precise enunciation of words was proof enough of her credentials as a woman of learning. Undoubtedly the Prophet felt Eliza had the positive attributes he sought in a teacher of youth. With Emma's approval, he invited Eliza to move in with his family. Flattered by the offer, and concerned to maintain herself, Eliza accepted the Smiths' hospitality and took up residence in their small home.

Over the following months, Eliza used her skills to create, or at least to help organize, a "select school for young ladies." It was the "Prophet's family school." Historians speculate that Eliza's school was the first in the church with a woman schoolteacher.

Eliza had not been long in Kirtland before she sent for the building committee of the nearly completed Kirtland Temple. She had seen the overwhelming sacrifices made by the Saints as they attempted to complete the structure they had been commanded to build. Impressed and sympathetic, she reflected on the patrimony she had received from her parents. She frankly asked the committee members if they would like a little money. Recording the response in her journal, Eliza noted, "They replied that they had a payment to make soon, and did not know where the means was coming from."

Then Eliza made an interesting statement showing an almost total lack of concern for economic dealings: "I do not recollect how much I gave them; however, it was sufficient to cover the present liability of the committee, who felt greatly relieved, and proposed to send me their note of hand for the amount."

Undoubtedly, Eliza had learned about the financial straits of the temple committee from either the Prophet or his wife Emma. The young woman had contributed from her heart. Shortly afterward, when given a loan note, she told the committee that she "did not want a note—they were welcome to the money."

Once Eliza had thrown her lot in with the Saints, all that she had would be theirs. This generosity was a central theme in her life. It is evident that her conversion had been complete, but persecution would yet test her stamina.

Chapter Two

A happy family life and a stimulating education shaped Eliza's childhood years. The Connecticut Western Reserve, part of the federal government's Revolutionary War reimbursement offered to those who had served in the military, made available cheap land and easy terms for men like Eliza's father, Oliver Snow. It was there, on the shore of Lake Erie in Ohio, that Eliza was born on January 21, 1804.

Eliza wrote of those early years: "I am the second of seven children—four daughters and three sons: all disciplined to habits of temperance, honesty, and industry; and our parents extended to us the best educational facilities attainable at that time, without preference to either sex."

That concluding phrase, "without preference to either sex," shaped Eliza's upbringing to give her a confidence in public life that few women of that era possessed.

Eliza was almost pretty, small-boned with delicate features. Hers was a precise manner, both in speech and actions. A misleading aura of fragility enhanced by her tendency to wear elaborately trimmed dresses disguised her tenacious spirit.

The Snows were farmers. Nevertheless the father performed civic duties and even kept an office where he engaged 10-year-old Eliza as secretary. Of that experience, Eliza wrote years later that it "proved of great benefit to myself and to others at different periods of my variegated life."

By her industrious mother, Eliza was instructed in the arts of homemaking. Her mother held the conviction that every young woman should have a practical knowledge of housekeeping. So naturally not only were Eliza and her sisters trained in housekeeping, but they learned cooking and needlework as well. So accomplished was the artistic Eliza that she won the Portage County Fair's prize award for "best manufactured leghorns," which were hats made of finely pleated bleached straw.

Perhaps most important in Eliza's early life was her schooling. The Snows paid for the finest available instruction on the frontier though it was not always consistent. At times Eliza's father, Oliver, was the instructor. But the children were never idle. Music, reading and tutoring occupied their leisure time.

"My apparently inherent fondness for reading was encouraged by my parents," Eliza wrote. "I was partial to poetical work and when very young frequently made attempts at imitation of the different styles of favorite authors."

Eliza must have been a precocious child. At school she had a unique method of preparing what she called her "dissertations." She would write up all her answers to assignments in rhyme. She claimed this elicited from her instructors "acknowledgments of inability to correct my articles through lack of poetical talent; and yet, my teachers were uniformly too indulgent to protest against my rhyming practice."

Indeed, Eliza had a talent for copying any poetical style of the day. She apparently could take song lyrics, newspaper poems, the classics or whatever and, by using the format of the poetry in print, similarly make up her own poetry. Once, while experimenting with a work, she copied the style of a "peculiar measure" from a war song that she had come across in a periodical. The rhyming article she wrote was humorous to Eliza, and she intended to turn it in to the instructor, a Presbyterian clergyman who would at times read the students' written work before the entire class. The day Eliza submitted her piece to the professor, however, he changed his procedure and asked that each student read his or her own work aloud instead. Eliza froze at her table, petrified at the idea. Since she thought her article to be "exceedingly amusing," she was certain it would create laughter in the classroom.

"I would break down if I attempted to read it," Eliza recalled. She could remain composed if the professor presented her work, but never if she had to read it herself.

"I tearfully told the Prof. I could not. But an equitable law must not be sacrificed to my timidity, and the Prof. compassionately helped me out of the dilemma by proposing to excuse me for the present, provided I would come the next morning, before the students assembled, and read it to him, to which I responded with all promptitude."

By the time Eliza grew aware of her writing's impact in school, she had already launched her career as a serious writer for journals and periodicals. For several years her articles appeared in publications "over an assumed name—wishing to be useful as a writer and unknown as an author."

During that phase of her career, "Narcissa" wrote with deep interest about the war between Greece and Turkey, concentrating on the fall of Missolonghi, a Greek town devastated by the Turks. Her article appeared just prior to the deaths of two great American patriots, John Adams and Thomas Jefferson, in 1826. When the press requested that she submit an entry to a writing contest, Eliza complied with a requiem for the former presidents. For her effort she received first prize, eight volumes of the popular *Godey's Lady's Book.*

Of that experience in journalism, Eliza summarized her talent with these words: "That 'men are born poets' is a common adage—I was born a patriot—at least, a warm feeling of patriotism inspired my thoughts as evinced in many of the early productions of my pen. I can even now recollect how, with beating pulse and with fond emotion I listened when but a small child, to narratives of the Revolution. My grandfather on my mother's side, when fighting for the freedom of his country, was taken prisoner, and confined in a dreary cell, and so scantily fed, that when a fellow prisoner, incarcerated with him, died from exhaustion, he reported him sick, in order to obtain the usual amount furnished for both—keeping him wrapped in his blanket as long as he dared to remain with a dead body. This with many other incidents of Revolutionary sufferings recounted by my grandparents, so deeply impressed my mind, that, as I grew up to womanhood, I fondly cherished a pride for the Flag which so proudly waved o'er the graves of my brave and valiant ancestors."

From her earliest years on, Eliza was taught from the Bible. Her parents, Baptists in those times, were according to Eliza's recollections "free from bigotry and intolerance." So quick-minded and attentive to memorization was Eliza that in her Sabbath School classes, she could fix in her mind and recite up to seven chapters of the gospels at a lesson. She later said of her Bible training, "When studying those interesting narratives, my mind, many times, was filled with reflections of the deepest type, and my heart yearned for the gifts and manifestations of which those ancient Apostles testified. Sometimes I wished I had lived when Jesus Christ was on the earth, that I might have witnessed the power of God manifested through the Gospel. . . ."

At last, the sensitive, eloquent young woman found that mighty spirit in Kirtland.

Four months after Eliza's arrival in Kirtland, the temple construction drew to completion. Eliza felt a sense of achievement for her donation of monies to help meet the construction loan payments. Later, she received a house and lot from the committee in exchange for her note. The lot, located near the temple, included a fresh-water spring, an orchard of fruit trees and a house large enough for two families. Eventually, Eliza rented out one-half of the house and moved her widowed sister into the remaining half.

To her, the temple was the focal point of excitement. Its dedication held unforgettable memories, not only for Eliza but for the hundreds who also attended. From that point on, dates and events would be remembered as taking place before or after the dedication of the Kirtland Temple.

Construction on the temple had commenced in June, 1833. The dedication took place just short of three years later, on March 27, 1836. The members had started with little more than hope. But by using every available resource, including their donations of fine china, which was crushed and mixed with mortar to give sparkle to the building's outside walls, the Saints accomplished the near back-breaking commitment. After all, everyone knew it was a commandment from God that they construct the temple. The edifice was not a large structure considering the awesome size of cathedrals and mosques around the world. Yet in Western America at that time, the building— eighty feet long by fifty-nine feet wide, with a tower at one end reaching a hundred and ten feet high—stood out for its imposing size.

On that late March day in 1836, every member who could attend assembled in the interior of the newly finished structure, in which the heavy canvas partition drapes had been rolled up to allow an open-hall view of the ranks of priesthood holders and ladies. The moment was electric.

Eliza, taking copious notes of the entire proceedings, graphically related the start of the dedication: "At nine o'clock, President Sidney Rigdon [Joseph Smith's counselor] commenced the services of that great and memorable day, by reading the ninety-sixth and twenty-fourth Psalms; 'Ere long the vail [sic] will be rent in twain,' etc. was sung by the choir, and after President Rigdon had addressed the throne of grace in fervent prayer, 'O happy souls who pray,' etc., was sung.

"President Rigdon then read. At one point, as he reviewed the toils and privations of those who had labored in rearing the walls of that sacred edifice, he drew tears from many eyes, saying, there were those who had wet those walls with their tears, when, in the silent shades of the night, they were praying to the God of heaven to protect them, and stay the unhallowed hands of ruthless spoilers, who had uttered a prophesy, when the foundation was laid, that the walls should never be erected."

Following Sidney Rigdon's two-and-a-half-hour discourse, he presented Joseph Smith, Jr., as "prophet, seer and revelator." All those assembled rose to their feet as a spontaneous sustaining vote was cast for their prophet. After a twenty-minute intermission, Joseph Smith, Jr., stood at the pulpit expounding a moment. Then he requested a formal sustaining vote by the congregation, the members' solemn witness that they would give their visible support. Everyone rose. Following music by the choir, the Prophet read a dedicatory prayer, and Eliza recorded verbatim every word of the 12-page hand-lettered prayer which the Prophet had written out prior to the meeting.

Following the dedication, the choir sang, "The Spirit of God

Like A Fire." Then came the standing congregation's hosanna shout, rendered with uplifted hands by the assemblage. More than 400 Saints shouted in unison, "Hosanna—hosanna— hosanna—to God and the lamb—amen—amen, and amen."

Heavenly manifestations followed. Many recorded in their journals that they saw angels. Eliza did not say *she* saw angels. But what she did record seemed appropriate for that moment: "Angels appeared to some, while a sense of divine presence was realized by all present, and each heart was filled with 'joy inexpressible and full of glory.'"

Eliza entered into an interesting pattern of behavior during the weeks that followed the temple's dedication. It became customary for her, as well as others, to visit the temple often to gain greater insight into its workings. The Kirtland Temple had not been constructed as a place to do vicarious baptisms for the dead, nor to perform any of the ordinances associated with later temples. The main business in the temple was worship and exhortation from the pulpit by key orators. The edifice also provided meeting areas in the draped hall for the presidency and priesthood quorums.

Through her worship at the temple, Eliza began to develop a talent for speaking in tongues.

In the earliest years of the restored church, this phenomenon had frequently been enjoyed among the more devout members, and rightly so. The Lord had promised that the gifts of the Spirit would follow His believers. From the time at age 14 of Joseph Smith's own remarkable visitation by God the Father and His Son, Jesus Christ, other individuals frequently received personal spiritual experiences.

Though not recorded in Eliza's journal, Joseph Smith and Oliver Cowdery had been privileged to receive a vision together at the temple dedication, in which Jesus Christ appeared to accept the temple as His house. The Lord's visit was followed by that of Moses, Elias and Elijah, all bestowing keys of authority on the Prophet and his assistant.

Surely Eliza was an eager observer as one after another of her associates received the gift of tongues, singing, prophesying, blessing one another in the language used by Adam to converse with God. Eliza must have read again and again the words Moroni engraved on the gold plates, later translated and known

16

as the *Book of Mormon*, just before he sealed the record to be preserved for that generation:

"And again I exhort you, my brethren," he wrote, "that ye deny not the gifts of God, for they are many; and they come from the same God. And there are different ways that these gifts are administered; but it is the same God who worketh all in all; and they are given by the manifestations of the Spirit of God unto men, to profit them. For behold, to one is given by the Spirit of God, that he may teach the word of wisdom; And to another, that he may teach the word of knowledge by the same Spirit; And to another, exceeding great faith; And to another, the gifts of healing by the same Spirit; And again, to another, that he may work mighty miracles; And again, to another, that he may prophesy concerning all things; And again, to another, the beholding of angels and ministering spirits; And again, to another, all kinds of tongues; And again to another, the interpretation of languages and of divers kinds of tongues. And all these gifts come by the Spirit of Christ; and they come unto every man severally according as he will."

Perhaps Eliza wondered initially about the propriety of speaking in tongues. The Corinthians of old had wondered also, for the Apostle Paul had sent them a lengthy epistle concerning that and other gifts. "If therefore the whole church be come together in one place," Paul said, "and all speak with tongues, and there come in those that are unlearned, or unbelievers, will they not say that ye are mad? . . . How is it brethren? When ye come together, every one of you hath a psalm, hath a doctrine, hath a tongue, hath a revelation, hath an interpretation. Let all things be done unto edifying. . . . Wherefore, brethren, covet to prophesy, and forbid not to speak with tongues. Let all things be done decently and in order."

If indeed she was ever ill at ease with such spiritual activity, Eliza soon became not only accustomed to, but thrilled by the gift of speaking in tongues.

Apparently, however, the prophet Joseph Smith felt that the Saints were becoming too preoccupied with exercising the gift of tongues. On one occasion he said, "Be not so curious about tongues. The gifts of God are all useful in their places, but when they are applied to that which God does not intend, they prove an injury, a snare, and a curse instead of a blessing." Consequently, he placed a limitation on the Saints' speaking in tongues.

One day a month the members of the growing church fasted, abstaining from food and water for 24 hours, in order to gain greater spirituality. Joseph indicated that only at the last hour of worship in the temple on that monthly fast day could they speak in tongues.

The Prophet's caution notwithstanding, Eliza was exhilarated by her newly found spiritual gift. Always obedient, she restrained herself for the present. But never had an experience offered her such joy as that—the privilege and ability to speak and interpret the language of Adam.

Chapter Three

In the autumn of 1836, Eliza traveled home to Mantua to visit her parents, themselves church members by that time. The young woman must have realized at the time of her return home that she would never again be content to live away from the main body of the Saints. Yet the thought of seeing her family, and of sharing her testimony, must have appealed to her. Eliza had left Kirtland for Mantua at the close of the school term. At home she became the center of attention: "Friends and acquaintances flocked around me to enquire about the 'strange people' with whom I was associated. I was exceedingly happy in testifying of what I had both seen and heard, until the 1st of January 1837 . . ."

When Eliza returned to Kirtland in January to teach the Prophet's children and to live in his home again, conditions were not as she had left them. No longer was the temple the great spiritual bastion of Kirtland. A change was creeping into the lives of the Saints—a spirit of dissention that would eventually destroy the idyllic atmosphere of former days in that wooded city. In the meantime, however, Eliza enjoyed her association with Joseph. From the beginning, she held strong feelings for the

Prophet. Her deep love for the man must have been difficult to quell.

Describing that time, she wrote, "By solicitation, on my return I resided in the family of Joseph Smith, and taught his family school, and had ample opportunity to mark his 'daily walk and conversation,' as a prophet of God; and the more I became acquainted with him, the more I appreciated him as such. His lips ever flowed with instruction and kindness, and, although very forgiving, indulgent, and affectionate in his temperament, when his God-like intuition suggested that the welfare of his brethren, or the interests of the kingdom of God demanded it, no fear of censure—no love of approbation could prevent his severe and cutting rebuke."

Joseph, the unpolished Prophet—he had the power and majesty of a true leader, though lacking in all forms of refinement. Eliza, the cultured lady—she possessed a polish and poise Joseph would learn from. Surely his heart was moved to touch her heart, knowing as he did that God had commanded him even at that early date to take other wives. For Eliza, Joseph's attraction, beyond their stimulating conversations, was "his expansive mind," which "grasped the great plan of salvation and solved the mystic problem of man's destiny."

Eliza undoubtedly felt that her admiration for the Prophet was purely platonic, that for her even to entertain any but the noblest feelings of brotherly love for Joseph would have violated her standards and reduced her high-minded admiration to something sordid and base. So she continued her teaching and aimed her devotion toward her brother, Lorenzo, whose involvement in the missionary activities of the church gave his sister a sense of pride in family that never ceased.

Eliza's younger brother Lorenzo held a very special place in her affections. Eliza's adoration of this brother, ten years her junior, had a maternal quality, going beyond the usual bonds of sibling affection. Eliza cared for Lorenzo as if she were his mother, dearest friend and confidante.

Lorenzo had been attending nearby Oberlin College. For Eliza, the fact that her younger brother was in college at all was a major victory. Earlier, Lorenzo had decided on a military career, a decision that had filled Eliza with concern: "I feared lest in the course of human events his path might lead to the battle field, and his earthly career prematurely close on a gory bed. I frequently plead [sic], entreated, and at times exhausted my stock of persuasion, but without effect." Or so she thought at the time.

Because Eliza felt Lorenzo was determined to pursue a military career, she consented to tailor a military uniform befitting her brother. Her sewing skills had not left her: "I made the suit—it was beautiful, magnificent, and my brother donned it with as much, if not of military pride, of self-satisfaction as ever Napoleon won a battle..."

The issue of military service was finally resolved when Lorenzo's more rational side took over and he listened to his sister's pleading. He hung up the uniform and returned to Oberlin as Eliza left for Kirtland, early in 1836.

On his walk to Oberlin, Lorenzo traveled with the splendid Mormon, David W. Patten, one of the firm missionaries of the restored church. Lorenzo, although aware of the Mormonism his family had embraced, often referred back to that conversation with Patten as one of the "trivial occurrences in human life which have an indelible trace." What he meant was that David W. Patten taught him that the Mormons had the true gospel of Jesus Christ. But the young man was not ready to be baptized.

Oberlin College was then a Presbyterian school and Lorenzo, a bright student, had quickly sized up the institution. In one of his many letters to Eliza he noted, "If there is nothing better than is found here in Oberlin College, good bye to all religions."

Eliza responded by begging him to come to Kirtland at the end of his school term. Always happy to please his sister, he went. He studied Hebrew and listened daily to Joseph Smith. Of that experience Eliza wrote, "While he studied the dead languages of the ancient Hebrews, his mind also drank in, and his heart became imbued with the living faith of the everlasting Gospel..."

Lorenzo entered the waters of baptism in June, 1836. By the following spring, he was on the road "without purse or scrip," preaching to people throughout the Ohio countryside.

Eliza had moved out of the Smith household by then, for her parents had bought a fine home a mile south of the Kirtland Temple. The move made it possible for all the Snow family to be together at home again. Yet the Snows' home as well as the Smiths' and others would be temporary residences because of the rapidly changing financial conditions in Kirtland.

The summer of 1837 proved financially disastrous for land speculators. Many members of the church had delved into the risky business of speculation and when the "panic" of '37 hit Kirtland, as it did the rest of the nation, those members lost money. Many felt Joseph to be a fallen prophet because he had not foreseen the panic and had been associated with the Kirtland bank.

Eliza witnessed a visible change in some of the people she knew, and wrote, "A spirit of speculation had crept into the hearts of some of the Twelve, and nearly, if not every quorum was more or less infected. Most of the Saints were poor, and now prosperity was dawning upon them—the Temple was completed, and in it they had been recipients of marvelous blessings, and many who had been humble and faithful to the performance of every duty—ready to go and come at every call of the Priesthood, were getting haughty in their spirits, and lifted up in the pride of their hearts. As the Saints drank in the love and spirit of the world, the Spirit of the Lord withdrew from their hearts, and they were filled with pride—pretended that they constituted the church, and claimed that the Temple belonged to them, and even attempted to hold it."

Kirtland's temple became the focal point of contention. Because most of the leading church authorities had been financially affected by speculation, they constituted a body of dissatisfied Saints. Not all turned on the Prophet, but a sufficient number did to create a powerful anti-Prophet group. These members claimed to be the legal body governing the church, and their aim was to secure all church properties, beginning with the temple.

Warren Parrish, according to Eliza, "had been a humble, successful preacher of the gospel," but he soon became the spokesperson for the apostate group of dissidents. At one point, armed with a pistol and a bowie knife, he even led a band of the dissidents into the temple. Eliza recorded the scene the Sabbath morning on which Warren Parrish and others tried to usurp authority in the opening services and literally take over the temple:

"Soon after the usual opening services, one of the brethren on the west stand arose, and just after he commenced to speak, one on the east interrupted him. Father Smith, presiding, called to order—he told the apostate brother that he should have all the time he wanted, but he must wait his turn—as the brother on the west took the floor and commenced first to speak, he must not be interrupted. A fearful scene ensued—the apostate speaker becoming so clamorous, that Father Smith called for the police to take that man out of the house, when Parrish, John Boynton, and others drew their pistols and bowie-knives, and rushed down from the stand into the congregation; J. Boynton saying he would blow out the brains of the first man who dared to lay hands on him. Many in the congregation, especially women and children, were terribly frightened—some tried to escape from the confusion by jumping out of the windows. Amid screams and shrieks, the policemen, in ejecting the belligerents, knocked down a stovepipe, which fell helter-skelter among the people; but, although bowie-knives and pistols were wrested from their owners, and thrown hither and thither to prevent disastrous results, no one was hurt, and after a short, but terrible scene to be enacted in a Temple of God, order was restored, and the services of the day proceeded as usual."

The next day Joseph Smith, Sr., affectionately known as Father Smith, and 16 others were arrested on a complaint filed by the belligerents. The group was charged with riot and bound over to the court. Eliza was subpoenaed as a witness to testify, but after she appeared she thought the whole court scene was "as amusing as the Temple scene was appalling."

Eliza simply refused to take the matter seriously. No one in his or her right mind, she thought, would convict a man such as the father of the Prophet Joseph. "The idea of such a man as Father Smith—so patriarchal in appearance—so circumspect in deportment and dignified in his manner, being guilty of a riot, was at once ludicrous and farcical to all same minded persons." The judge dismissed the case with "no cause for action." Father Smith and the 16 others were soon free.

But the harassment and persecution were just beginning for the Prophet and his family—and for Eliza as well. The Snows were able to ease some of it, however, through their ever-ready hospitality.

By late autumn, 1837, Joseph Smith and Sidney Rigdon fled Kirtland. Yet their departure for Far West, Missouri, failed to check the persecution. The Prophet's father was once again sought by the law on a state warrant for his arrest. He was able to escape through the able assistance of the local constable, a non-participating Mormon named Luke Johnson, who felt it was a shame to arrest such a kindly person. Johnson told the trusting patriarch where he could hide: "Go up to Esquire Snow's—he is a quiet man, and no one will think of going there for you."

It was midnight when the Snows opened their door to the knock of Father Smith. The next day, Eliza happened to meet Luke Johnson. The two conversed about the escape, and Luke asked how the older man was doing at the Snows' home, if he had reached it "all right." Later, in parting, Luke told Eliza, "Father Smith will bless me for it," referring to Luke's part in the escape, "all the days of his life."

It was true. Luke Johnson later returned to the church and died in Salt Lake City.

After such episodes, conditions at Kirtland became intolerable for most of the faithful members. The Snows decided by April of 1838 that they too would sell their property and, in one giant caravan of family and close friends, follow the main body of the church to Far West, Missouri, where they hoped to find peace. This would be the first of several forced moves made by Eliza and her family. She would yet see more trying conditions, but firmly she believed in the gospel and its leaders.

Chapter Four

The trek from Kirtland to Far West lasted two and a half months. The Snows led a company of 21 persons, among them all but one sister of Eliza. The group traveled in wagons hauled by horse and ox teams. It was a wet spring. A hundred miles east of Far West, Lorenzo became ill. He had had charge of one of his father's teams, but he could no longer drive it, so great was the pain caused him by the bouncing wagon. Eliza recalled, "For nearly one hundred miles he suffered such a racking pain in his head that when we traveled I held it as steady as possible to prevent excruciating suffering being produced by the motion of the wagon."

The first home the company came upon in Far West was that of their good friend, Sidney Rigdon. Concerned over Lorenzo's illness, Elder Rigdon insisted that the sick young man remain. The elder had built a fine log structure, one of the finest in the settlement, with awnings and a water pump. There Lorenzo would stay, in Eliza's able care, while the Snows found their own home.

The Snows had decided to purchase property in a settlement

30 miles from Far West which the Prophet had named Adam-ondi-Ahman. They left to complete their arduous journey the following morning, Oliver Snow promising to return after he settled his family and considerable livestock on the new lands he hoped to purchase.

Thus began a vigil by Eliza that she would never forget. "My brother grew worse—the fever increased until he became quite delirious." Eliza tried to obtain medicine from a Dr. Avord, a church member. But the physician seemed puzzled by Lorenzo's illness. Eliza grew impatient with Dr. Avord when he refused her the medicine she had requested. She asked the doctor for his bill, signaling that she was fed up with his medical treatment of her brother. "The idea struck him at once that this request signified non-attendance, and he was very angry and tried to frighten me concerning my brother's condition, by telling me that his skill was needed more than when he first saw the patient."

The doctor at length presented his bill and left the sickroom, only to seat himself day after day under the Rigdons' awning to shade himself. Never once did he glance in on the sick young man.

The Rigdons apparently were not in agreement with Eliza's dismissal of the doctor. Eliza later summed up her feeling on that matter, writing, "I realized that the family of Sidney Rigdon, himself included, at that time had more faith in medical treatment than in the healing ordinances, and they all thought me to blame for discharging the physician."

Eliza put her complete trust in God. With the faith and determination that would forever distinguish her from the average, she prayed while nursing her dearly loved brother. It took days, but the fever abated, Lorenzo regained consciousness and two weeks later Eliza sent word to her father to come fetch them. A wagon with a feather bed arrived to take the two to Davies County at Adam-ondi-Ahman.

In Adam-ondi-Ahman, Oliver Snow had purchased a "plantation," paying for it entirely with cash. On the land stood a double log house with a passageway about three feet wide between the two buildings. Possessing cash, stock and a solid family background, the Snows appeared to be what they had always been, successful people.

Within a few months, many of the non-Mormon Missouri settlers living nearby in crude cabins took offense at the Snows and other Saints as the Mormons began to prosper. A spirit of mobocracy raised its ugly head. The Snows had heard about confrontations in other Mormon settlements, but the first incident to alarm them in their new home was the violent shooting of the family watchdog by mobbers.

At first, mob action had taken more the form of verbal threats rather than any physical force. But the mob wanted the Mormons out. As tension built, the Snows prepared for the worst.

"One night at about 11 o'clock," wrote Eliza of one strange event in the growing atmosphere of fear, "we all were suddenly aroused from sleep by the discharge of fire arms, accompanied with loud shouts, apparently about a mile distant. We supposed that our enemies had commenced their depredations by putting their threats into execution, and were making an attack on our people, and the probability was that they would visit us in turn. We immediately began to prepare for defense by barricading the doors and windows, and distributing among all the members of the family such weapons for protection as were available, viz: one sword, two or three guns, pitchforks, axes, shovels, and tongs, etc. We proposed that mother take her choice, and she thought that she could do the best execution with the shovel. With no small degree of anxiety, not only for ourselves, but also in behalf of our friends situated at the point from which the exciting sounds proceeded, we kept up a sleepless watch until morning, when intelligence was brought, explaining the cause of the night alarm, as follows: A company of our brethren had been to a distant settlement to accomplish some business requisite in consequence of threatened mob violence, and on their return, having peacefully and successfully accomplished their object, discharged their fire arms, accompanied with a shout expressive of their happy success—resulting in our false alarm and subsequent amusement."

However, soon afterward when a mob stormed the Snow home, there was real cause for alarm.

In a concerted move to stir up the countryside against the Mormon settlers, neighbors to the Snows and other Mormons one day pulled off a trick that would generate almost certain violence. Leaving their homes in great haste, to the surprise of the Mormons, "those neighbors fled from the place, as if driven by a mob, leaving their clocks ticking, dishes spread for their meal, coffee-pots boiling, etc."

The neighbors made it appear as if the Mormons had driven them out. Their scheme succeeded, and the tale of supposed persecution aroused the surrounding inhabitants and reached all the way to the governor. He, in turn, called out the state militia and ultimately issued the infamous "extermination order."

There seemed no recourse but to obey the governor's order for the Mormons to leave the state within 10 days. He promised protection during those fateful 10 days, though Eliza wondered which was worse, the threats of the mob or of the posse of crazed militia who ostensibly guarded the Mormons as they prepared to leave. During that preparation time, the former occupant of the Snows' plantation returned to the house and inquired how soon the Snows intended to depart. He was forced to leave without an answer. Though he had resisted the vulture-like query, Oliver Snow soon sacrificed the land and buildings to the mob.

It was on the tenth and final day of the governor's grace period that the Snows and all the other Mormons in the settlement began the cold journey back to Far West, trudging over snow-covered roads to the community 30 miles distant to rendezvous with the main body of the Saints.

"After assisting in the arrangements for the journey, and shivering with cold, in order to warm my aching feet, I walked until the teams overtook me," Eliza wrote.

She made some caustic remarks about that walk in the snow, mentioning that she "met one of the so-called militia, who accosted me with, 'Well, I think this will cure you of your faith!' Looking him steadily in the eye, I replied, 'No, sir, it will take more than *this* to cure me of my faith.' His countenance suddenly fell, and he responded, 'I must confess, you are a better soldier than I am.' I passed on, thinking that unless he was above the average of his fellows in that section, I was not highly complimented by his confession."

It took two strenuous days of travel for the Snows to reach Far West. The first night on the road they lodged at a halfway house, a log building which lacked chinking between the logs. The Snows figured the chinking had been burned out by the owners, the Littlefields, before they had left for Far West. Still, the Snows' party hoped for safety, though warmth they were denied. The north wind blew all night long through the open cracks, which Eliza described as large enough for a cat to crawl through. About 80 people were squeezed into the structure, with very little space for anyone to lie down. Eliza and her sister sat on either side of their mother, who stretched out on the floor to sleep.

The evening meal had consisted of frozen bread dipped in fresh cow's milk to help thaw it. Breakfast seemed easier because many had already departed before the Snows were ready to go. Left almost by themselves, the family crowded up close to the fire and toasted bread and thawed meat which had frozen solid on the journey.

At Far West, news of the Prophet's arrest and imprisonment shocked the Snows. Eliza visited the Prophet's wife, Emma, only to learn that that pitiable woman had not only watched her husband being dragged to prison, but had stood helpless while militia had plundered the cabin, leaving her and her small children with little more than parched corn. According to Eliza's recollections, "desolation seemed inscribed on everything but the hearts of the faithful saints. In the midst of affliction, they trusted in God."

The Snows, like many others, were reduced to living on bread made of corn that the women of the family grated on implements fashioned from tin pails and stovepipes. Even though the family had a store of wheat, there was no place to grind it. Of this trying period, Eliza wrote:

> 'Twas autumn—Summer's melting breath was gone,
> And Winter's gelid blast was stealing on;
> To meet its dread approach, with anxious care
> The houseless saints were struggling to prepare;
> When round about a desperate mob arose,
> Like tigers waking from a night's repose;
> They came like hordes from nether shades let loose—
> Men without hearts, just fit for Satan's use!
> With wild, demoniac rage they sallied forth,
> Resolved to drive the saints of God from earth.
> Hemm'd in by foes—deprived the use of mill,
> Necessity inspires their patient skill;
> Tin-pails and stove-pipe, from their service torn,
> Are changed to graters to prepare the corn,

That nature's want may barely be supplied—
They ask no treat, no luxury beside.
But, where their shelter? Winter hastens fast;
Can tents and wagons stem this northern blast?

With the arrest of the Prophet, the Missouri officials relaxed their stance toward the Mormons somewhat. The Snows spent the remainder of that winter tented in the vicinity of Far West. Of those several bitterly cold months Eliza is silent in her record. Somehow the family made it to the 5th of March, 1839, when Oliver Snow and his sons hitched teams and oxen to wagons, rounded up the livestock and followed the vanguard of Saints east, exiting Missouri.

The family had never before seen such disrespect for civil people as they encountered from the hostile Missourians who drove them out. Eliza, in her frustration and sorrow, recounted in detail one incident which took place on the eastward trek from Far West.

"After a night of rain which turned to snow and covered the ground in the morning, we thawed our tent, which was stiffly frozen, by holding and turning it alternately before a blazing fire until it could be folded for packing; and, all things put in order, while we all shook with the cold, we started on. As the sun mounted upwards, the snow melted, and increased the depth of the mud with which the road before us had been amply stocked, and rendered travel almost impossible. The teams were puffing, and the wagons dragging so heavily that we were all on foot, tugging along as best we could, when an elderly gentleman, on horseback, overtook us, and, after riding alongside for some time, apparently absorbed in deep thought, as he (after inquiring who we were) watched the women and girls, men and boys, teams and wagons, slowly wending our way up a long hill, en route from our only earthly homes, and, not knowing where we should find one, he said emphatically, 'If I were in your place, I should want the Governor of the State hitched at the head of my teams.' I afterward remarked to my father that I had not heard as sensible a speech from a stranger since entering the State. I never saw that gentleman afterwards, but have from that time cherished a filial respect for him..."

The state of Missouri closed its gates behind the Snows when the family reached the ferries at the Mississippi and started across to Quincy, Illinois.

That bitter journey east would draw an exacting emotional toll from the Snow family, a cost beyond the financial and physical hardships they had already had to bear. Eliza would not accept such treatment from citizens of the United States without lashing out at them in her writings. The Mormons' persecutors had not begun to dampen her spirit and love for what she knew to be the gospel of Christ. Her parents, on the other hand, had reached a point of mental exhaustion in defending their belief. In the future they would see spiritual things differently than some of their children. Forced evacuations from two states had left their marks on the elder Snows, indelible scars that reflected the erosion of their faith.

Chapter Five

By 1841, Eliza declared her home to be Nauvoo. The Illinois city represented to her the centermost place of Zion, and she treasured the marvelous feeling of community there after the nightmare of Missouri. Nauvoo meant "city beautiful," according to the Prophet Joseph. By 1842 the city would develop from a swampy, malaria-infected bend in the Mississippi River to a graceful, pleasant western town visited by hundreds who journeyed up and down the great Mississippi River.

Said one writer, "Nauvoo was bidding fair to become the queen of the West." Everyone, especially Eliza, felt that Nauvoo, the "second Zion," would become not only queen of the West, but the city that would set the pattern for a New Jerusalem.

Though set in beautiful country, Nauvoo's environs did not yield to human habitation without a fight. Eliza wrote, "The location of the city of Nauvoo was beautiful, but the climate was so unhealthy that none but Latter-day Saints, full of faith, trusting in the power of God, could have established that city. Chills and fever was [sic] the prevailing disease. Nothwithstanding we had this to contend with, through the blessing of

God on the indefatigable exertions of the saints, it was not long before Nauvoo prompted the envy and jealousy of many of the adjacent inhabitants, and, as the 'accuser of the brethren' never sleeps, we had many difficulties to meet...."

But she, like the other persecution-wearied Saints, was enthralled with the prospect of building a magnificent city.

Eliza had made several moves after leaving western Missouri but prior to settling permanently in Nauvoo: "We started *en route* for Illinois, landing in Quincy; we stopped there a short time, and from there our father moved to Warren County, in the same state; from there to La Harpe, where Lorenzo found us, thence to Commerce, afterward called Nauvoo."

The family had separated following a brief stay in Quincy. Eliza with her sister Leonora had moved briefly to Lima, where they found work as seamstresses. Next to schoolteaching, seamstress work was the occupation Eliza understood best, and she seemed to have a real talent for the skill she had learned from her mother.

In Lima, 30 miles south of Nauvoo, Eliza, her sister and her sister's two small daughters lived in an upstairs room rented out by a family who had little, if any, love for the Mormons, though they expressed friendship and warmth toward their tenants, the Snows.

While preparing for bed one evening, Eliza and Leonora could not help overhearing a conversation taking place beneath them in the parlor. Their landlord was shouting his disgust for the Mormons to his guests. According to Eliza, "We were obliged to hear bitter aspersions against those whom we knew to be the best people on earth. Frequently our host, after vilely traducing our people, of whom he knew nothing, suddenly changed his tone, and boasted of the 'two noble women' [Eliza and Leonora] he had in his house. 'No better women ever lived,' he insisted."

Eliza recorded her thoughts of that experience in poetry, some of which was later published. Among the poems was the work "Prejudice, What Is It?"

Eliza's stay in Lima was cut short because in July of 1839, Sidney Rigdon sent for her. He wanted her to move into his home and set up a school. Eliza gladly consented. She moved as readily to Nauvoo as she had to Kirtland. Again she was surrounded by dear friends as she resumed her position as instructor and poet.

Consideration being inherently a part of her nature, Eliza also concerned herself with the Rigdon family. When Sidney's mother, who lived with them, passed away early in October of that year, Eliza was by her side.

The devout woman had admired Sidney Rigdon from the time he was a Campbellite preacher, and she would grow much concerned some two years after her stay in his home when his views conflicted with those of the Prophet. In her journal, Eliza later recorded her hopes for Sidney's spiritual welfare: "How it would rejoice my heart to see him once more standing firmly in the dignity of his station and strengthening the hands of those who are struggling against every kind of opposition for the cause of God."

During the winter of 1839, Oliver Snow came to Nauvoo to fetch Eliza because her mother was ill, her suffering still the result of the prolonged exposure and hardships in Missouri. Eliza remained with her family, moving with them to La Harpe in 1840 and finally to Nauvoo in the spring of 1841.

Times were turbulent once again for the Mormons. John C. Bennett, a bright, energetic man who had quickly become a confidant to the Prophet when the Mormons had settled Nauvoo, "defected from the faith" by the time Eliza moved to the bustling city. The accounts Bennett spread abroad of licentious "spiritual wifery" were causing a stir in surrounding settlements. Moreover, Joseph was not only fighting the dissention Bennett sowed, but he also had to contend with outside forces set on punishing him for alleged crimes in Missouri. Into this turmoil Eliza returned, full of hope and the desire to be of service.

Little time passed before her talents were put to good use. In March, 1842, the Prophet established the Relief Society, after several of the leading women of the church had presented to him a proposal that the sisters organize to help the needy and distressed. Eliza was elected the Relief Society's first secretary to serve under Emma Smith, who was elected to act as president of the newly formed organization.

Martha McBride Knight, one of the charter members who attended the first Relief Society meeting, recalled, "Joseph Smith had to leave before the meeting was dismissed, so he took his watch out of his pocket and laid it on the table by Eliza R. Snow, the secretary of the meeting, and said, 'Begin your meetings on time and close them on time.' He left the watch on the table and Eliza R. Snow kept it in her possession until her death."

For a brief period of time Eliza and Emma made a dynamic team. Under the careful tutelage of the Prophet Joseph, together with the help of counselors Sarah M. Cleveland and Elizabeth Ann Whitney, they carefully defined the purposes and duties of the women's organization. There was much need of their services among the struggling Saints. Relief Society members sewed clothing for missionaries and temple construction workers. They secured temporary homes for the gathering Saints who arrived almost daily from all parts of the United States and Europe. And the women taught homemaking skills and assisted in times of illness, childbirth and death, soon growing to be justly regarded by their grateful beneficiaries as angels of mercy.

While Eliza was feverishly caught up in service to her people, her family—after being in Nauvoo barely a year—once more planned a move. Still searching for a farm to compare with the one he had left behind in Mantua, Ohio, Oliver Snow determined to try his luck in Walnut Grove, a small community some 50 miles east of Nauvoo.

Oliver's decision placed Eliza in a quandry. She longed to remain in Nauvoo, so thoroughly a part of the society of the Saints, but if her parents moved away, she would once more be without a home or a secure means of support.

She recorded the solution to her problem in a journal given her three months earlier by her friend Sarah M. Kimball. When viewed from the broader scope that history provides, her entry is a fascinating understatement.

"City of Nauvoo, June 29th, 1842. This is a day of much interest to my feelings," she wrote. "Reflecting on past occurrences, a variety of thoughts have presented themselves to my mind with regard to events which have chas'd each other in rapid succession in the scenery of human life."

In veiled and cryptic language, Eliza was recording her eternal marriage to the Prophet Joseph as a plural wife.

She later wrote: "The Prophet Joseph had taught me the principle of plural, or Celestial Marriage, and I was married to him for time and eternity. In consequence of the ignorance of most of the Saints, as well as people of the world, on the subject, it was not mentioned only privately between the few whose minds were enlightened on the subject."

There is no clear record of just when Joseph presented his concept of plural marriage to Eliza. He could have told her as early as the Kirtland period, for certainly Eliza was among those who knew the inner workings of the community of Kirtland, and later of Far West and Nauvoo. Thus, she had had ample opportunity to learn of the Prophet's concept. It is now recognized that some knew as early as the Kirtland period that Joseph had received a revelation on plural marriage, so it is possible that Eliza was privy to the doctrine even then.

Whether or not Joseph directly approached Eliza at Kirtland, he did teach the principle to her in the early days of Nauvoo. That she loved Joseph is an undisputed truth. She said of him in her later years that Joseph was "the choice of my heart and the crown of my life." What is more, his proposal of marriage offered to her more than financial security, more than the guarantee that she could remain in the bosom of the Saints. To Eliza, being sealed for time and eternity to a prophet of God meant eternal salvation at the highest level, even exaltation, if she and he remained pure and worthy.

Nothwithstanding all that her marriage meant to her, Eliza continued her journal entry with an aura of sadness.

"As an individual," she wrote, "I have not passed altogether unnoticed by Change, in reference to present circumstances and future prospects. Two weeks and two days have pass'd since an intimation was presented of my duty and privilege of remaining in the City of the saints in case of the removal of my father's family: one week and two days have transpired since the family left, and though I rejoice in the society of the saints, and the approbation of God; a lonely feeling will steal over me before I am aware, while I am contemplating the present state of society—the powers of darkness, and the prejudices of the human mind which stand array'd like an impregnable barrier against the work of God."

At first Eliza had been repulsed by the thought of entering into plural marriage: "The thought was very repugnant to my feelings, and in direct opposition to my educational prepossessions;..."

Her concern with plural marriage seemed to pivot on what

others would think as well as on an innate repugnance to such a radical departure from her traditional concept of marriage. Unquestionably, Eliza loved the Prophet. Her struggle was with the possibility that her marriage could become a source of public ridicule. In later years she wrote of her fears: "It seemed for awhile as though all the traditions, prejudices, and superstitions of my ancestry, for many generations, accumulated before me in one immense mass; but God, who had kept silence for centuries was speaking; I knew it, and had covenanted in the waters of baptism to live by every word of his, and my heart was still firmly set to do his bidding."

In other writings she mentioned that she had thought the practice "was a long way in the distance, beyond the period of my mortal existence." But when confronted with the announcement to her "that the 'set time' had come—that God had commanded his servants to establish the order..." Eliza seemed to be reconciled to the fact.

With that decision behind her, she placed in her orderly mind the new set of values. Eliza declared later, "I was sealed to the prophet, Joseph Smith, for time and eternity, in accordance with the celestial law of marriage which God had revealed, the ceremony being performed by a servant of the Most High—authorized to officiate in sacred ordinances. This, one of the most important events of my life, I have never had cause to regret."

Despite the spiritual and emotional significance of Eliza's and Joseph's marriage, however, there was no public display of Eliza's new relationship with the Prophet.

Her vague journal entry was probably necessary at the time, for the whole issue of polygamy was coming to a head. The tense emotional climate of Nauvoo and the fear that there would follow severe persecution left Eliza little choice.

She expressed her frustrations, as usual, in poetry. But because "this principle" she discussed in her verses referred to plural marriage, her poem was one of the few she wrote that was not published. With this brief explanation, she recorded the poem in her Nauvoo Journal:

"To stand still and see the salvation of God seems to be the only alternative for the present. While reflecting on the present, and its connexion [sic] with the future; my thoughts mov'd in the following strain:"

O, how shall I compose a thought
When nothing is compos'd?
How form ideas as I ought
On subjects not disclos'd?

If we are wise enough to know
To whom we should give heed—
Thro' whom intelligence must flow
The church of God to lead,

We have *one* grand position gain'd—
One point, if well possess'd—
If well established—well maintain'd,
On which the mind may rest.

This principle will bear us up—
It should our faith sustain,
E'en when from "trouble"'s reckless cup
The dregs, we have to drain.

What boots it then, tho' tempests howl
In thunders, round our feet—
Tho' human rage, and nature's scowl
By turns, we have to meet.

What though tradition's haughty mood
Deals out corroding wrongs;
And superstition's jealous brood
Stirs up the strife of tongues.

Eliza later wrote of that era in Nauvoo: "To narrate what transpired within the seven years in which we built and occupied Nauvoo, the beautiful, would fill many volumes. This is a history that never will, and never can, repeat itself. Some of the most important events of my life transpired within that brief term, in which I was married, and in which my husband, Joseph Smith, the prophet of God, sealed his testimony with his blood."

Historical records do not always detail where Eliza lived for the first few weeks following her marriage, but it seems clear that Joseph saw that she was provided for.

Her journal notation for August 14, 1842, sheds some light on her whereabouts: "Yesterday Mrs. [Emma] Smith sent for me, having previously given me the offer of a home in her house, by Miss A. Coles [Cowles], who call'd on me, on the 12th. Mrs. [Sarah] Cleveland having come to the determination of moving on to her lot; my former expectations were frustrated, but the

Lord has opened the path to my feet, and I feel dispos'd to acknowledge his hand in all things. This sudden, unexpected change in my location, I trust is for good; it seem'd to come in answer to my petitions to God to direct me in the path of duty according to his will."

Some historians are of the opinion that Eliza shared strictly a platonic relationship with the Prophet, that she was a wife in name only. She was 38 when she married Joseph, the very age of his first wife, Emma, at that time. Eliza was childless, it is true, but according to historian Donna Hill, "There is a persistent story that Eliza conceived a child by Joseph in the spring of 1844 but had a miscarriage." Documents exist which indicate that some of those women who married Joseph Smith as plural wives did bear children by him. And certainly other men who entered the order of polygamy formed strong, loving, physical relationships with all their wives. Some men were father to 30 or 40 or more children. Brigham Young had 56.

It is tempting to read unwritten meaning into some of Eliza's veiled journal entries such as the one recorded on October 10, 1843: "Yesterday returned from Nauvoo. The trial of Prest. Rigdon occupied that portion of the Conference which I attended. Some circumstances of very peculiar interest occur'd during my visit to the city. Everything connected with our affections is engraven on the heart, and needs not the perpetuating touch of the sculptor."

Whatever the personal relationship, both Eliza and Emma devoted their full energies to their prophet husband and to the church he had helped to restore. Eliza accompanied Emma to Quincy, Illinois, where together they held an audience with Governor Thomas Carlin seeking his assurance of protection for the Prophet. About a thousand of the women of Nauvoo had signed a petition affirming Joseph Smith's integrity. They wanted the state to extend safeguards to Joseph, who had had several attempts made upon his life and who had barely escaped arrest, time and again, by deputies out of Missouri.

According to Eliza, Governor Carlin received the women "with cordiality, and as much affability and politeness as his Excellency is master of, assuring us of his protection, by saying that the laws and Constitution of our country shall be his polar star in case of any difficulty."

Having been through the Missouri expulsion, however, Eliza did not accept the governor's word at face value. She wrote in her diary that day that the governor "manifested much friendship, and it remains for time and circumstance to prove the sincerity of his professions."

Later Eliza wrote a postscript about the audience and her skepticism about Governor Carlin: "But alas! Soon after our return, we learned that at the time of our visit, and while making protestations of friendship, the wily Governor was secretly conniving with the basest of men to destroy our leaders."

Two weeks after Emma and Eliza returned from speaking with the governor, Joseph Smith and his loyal guard, Porter Rockwell, were arrested, then released on a technicality. At that point, Joseph went into hiding to avoid re-arrest.

It was another of those turbulent times that tested the faith of the members. Eliza wrote:

> O God, thou God that rules on high
> Bow down thy ear to me;
> Listen, O Listen to my cry
> And hear my fervent plea.

At the time the Prophet went into hiding, his wife Emma was confined to her bed with the fever so prevalent in Nauvoo. Upon hearing of the Prophet's safe arrival at a secret location, Eliza wrote him a note in poetry:

> Prest Smith,
> Sir, for your consolation permit me to tell
> That your Emma is better—she soon will be well;
> Mrs. Durfee stands by her, night and day like a friend
> And is prompt every call—every wish to attend;
> Then pray for your Emma, but indulge not a fear
> For the God of our forefathers, smiles on us here.
>
> Thou hast found a seclusion—a lone solitude
> Where thy foes cannot find thee—where friends can't intrude;
> In its beauty and wildness, by nature design'd
> As a retreat from the tumult of all humankind,
> And estrang'd from society: How do you fare?
> May the God of our forefathers, comfort you there.
>
> It is hard to be exil'd! but be of good cheer
> Thou art destin'd to triumph: then like a chas'd deer

Hide yourself in the ravine, secure from the blast
Awhile, till the storm of their fury is past;
For your foes are pursuing and hunting you still
May the God of our forefathers screen you from ill.

That fall, Eliza also came down with the ague, an illness of chills and fevers that relentlessly persisted into winter. However, she recovered enough to open school on December 12, 1842: "This day commenced school-teaching in the Masonic Hall—the weather very cold and I shall never forget the kindness of Bishop Whitney, who opened the school by prayer after having assisted in preparing the room," she wrote.

Thirty-seven students ranging in age from 4 to 17 were her charges. Among them were four children of Joseph and Emma Smith, five of Newel and Elizabeth Whitney, two Partridge children, three Knights, and one of William Marks.

Commenting on the task of teaching during that winter of 1842, Eliza reflected: "In undertaking the arduous business with my delicate constitution, at this inclement season of the year, I was entirely governed by the wishes of Prest. and Mrs. Smith; trusting in God for strength to fulfill, and acknowledging his hand in this as well as in every other circumstance of my life; I believe he has a purpose to accomplish which will be for my good ultimately, inasmuch as I desire and aim to be submissive to the requirements of those whom he has plac'd in authority over me."

But life was never static for Eliza R. Snow. On February 11, 1843, Eliza made a brief note in her journal. It is interesting for what is *not* said: "Took board and had my lodging removed to the residence of br. Holmes."

It may be that the reason for her move was a simple one: Perhaps the Smith home was overcrowded. They were living at the time in the "Homestead," a four-room wooden house. Even with four children of their own at the time, the Smiths frequently took in homeless youngsters. Joseph's mother may have been living with them as well.

Eliza's abrupt change of address might also suggest that there was indeed a physical as well as a spiritual marriage between Eliza and Joseph and that Emma had become jealous. It is also possible that Emma Smith had not earlier been aware of their marriage at all.

It is a well established fact that Emma vacillated in her attitude toward plural marriage, especially where her husband was concerned. At times she would witness with apparent agreeability the marriages of Joseph to other women, then within hours she might threaten dire circumstances if the relationships were not dissolved.

It is not surprising, therefore, that Eliza suddenly left the Smith household in 1843 without preplanning her move. Several diary accounts shed a little more light on the event. They indicate that the Smiths had a family quarrel one night during which Emma pulled Eliza down the stairs by her hair and threw her out into the dark. Young Joseph, the Prophet's and Emma's eldest son, was troubled over the scene. Allen Joseph Stout, a bodyguard to the Prophet, took the boy back to bed with him in an effort to comfort him.

Later entries in Eliza's own journal indicate a continuing amicable relationship with Emma, however. Eliza noted that she closed her school in March in "the presence of Prest J. Smith, his lady" and others. She also indicated on June 27, 1843, that she called upon Emma following another arrest of Joseph to learn "...more particulars concerning the manner in which her husband was taken...."

That Emma knew sometime during that period that Joseph had married Eliza is certain. We have Eliza's word on it according to David McKay, father of President David O. McKay. In a letter to Mrs. James Hood in Glasgow, Scotland, David McKay wrote of asking Eliza R. Snow some pointed questions many years later. One in particular is pertinent here.

McKay: "I heard My Mother say that your full name was Eliza R. Snow Smith. How did you come by that last name?"

E.R.S.: "I was married to the Prophet Joseph Smith Jun."

McKay: "Did Emma Hale Smith know that you were married to her husband, Joseph Smith?"

E.R.S.: "Just as well as you know that you are sitting by my side in this Buggy."

Eliza frequently expressed her love for Joseph, but she couched her feelings in praise of the Prophet, rather than of her husband. She would yet talk of her deep love in later years when the Mormon community would be safely settled in the Rocky Mountains, but while in Nauvoo, the longing of her heart was never openly acknowledged.

At that time tributes to Joseph in poetry were acceptable in the Mormon journals, and Eliza covered reams of paper in praise and defense of the man she regarded as a peer of Jesus Christ. Surely the crowning moment of her life was her eternal marriage to Joseph, her prophet.

But the poetess was notably a patient person; she could wait the years it might take to satisfy her longings. And wait she would have to do, as events began to wrench and twist the Saints in their struggle to hold fast to their beautiful city, Nauvoo.

Chapter Six

Perhaps the greatest apprehension Eliza suffered in marrying Joseph came less than a year after their marriage when her brother, Lorenzo, returned from London. A tumult of emotions filled Eliza as she awaited the steamship ploughing its way to port at Nauvoo. Lorenzo had kept Eliza informed of all the excitement of his mission. He had been appointed counselor to Parley P. Pratt and was bringing with him 240 converts, many of them his own contacts who had joined the church in London while he presided over that city.

Expressing her excitement at standing on the wharf at Nauvoo opposite the post office building, craning her neck to see the steamship, Eliza wrote: "The time of arrival had been announced, and many hearts (mine not excepted) were anxiously and expectantly beating, and when the steamer came in sight, every eye was turned in the direction, and as it neared the landing, white handkerchiefs were waving along the shore, up and down, for a great distance. President Joseph Smith, with a large number of brothers and sisters, was present to greet our friends. . . ." It is easy to comprehend that the arrival of a company of Saints from Europe was hailed as an important event.

She continued, "The appearance of the 'Amaranth' as it came in sight, attracted the gaze of many eyes, but I then thought, and still think, that of all the crowd that watched its progress up the Mississippi, as it approached the wharf, no one felt a deeper interest than myself. Knowing that the steamer held a dear brother with whom, three years before, I parted for an indefinite period, I watched it coming, and the white handkerchiefs waving from its deck—perhaps one is his, and in a few moments I shall clasp the hand that waves it!"

Eliza revealed some of her puritan reserve when she noted, "Although I determined to appear to the bystanders undemonstrative..." In other words, she probably did not jump up and down shouting; rather, she likely fluttered her hankie in a very proper, ladylike manner. But her feelings were deep. Observed Eliza, "It may seem trivial to others, but that is one of the incidents in my life that has fastened indelibly in my memory."

The eager sister was turning about in the confusion, trying to spot Lorenzo, when the Prophet Joseph's brother, Hyrum, said to her, "Your brother has actually arrived." At last Lorenzo was home. Eliza wrote, "I have the inexpressible happiness of once again embracing a brother who had been absent nearly three years. I cannot describe the feelings which fill'd my bosom...."

Those feelings were divided. Eliza had no idea how her brother would react to the news that she had married the Prophet. "Not knowing how my brother would receive it, I did not feel at liberty, and did not wish to assume the responsibility of instructing him in the principle of plural marriage..." she wrote.

Within days after Lorenzo greeted his sister and had opportunities to chat with her, it became apparent that he was beginning to wonder at Eliza's silences and evasive language.

"I was forced, by his cool and distant manner, to feel that he was growing jealous of my sisterly confidence—that I could not confide in his brotherly integrity. I could not endure this— something must be done," an unhappy Eliza wrote.

She informed her husband of her distressful situation and asked him to speak with Lorenzo about it. Joseph accepted the challenge.

The occasion was not the first time Joseph had provided such direction. It seems logical that when the Prophet had first instructed Eliza in the law of Celestial Marriage, he likely told her of the trying time he personally had had accepting the doctrine as it was revealed, then commanded of him to perform. Eliza, describing how the Prophet explained the new order to others, lets us in on some of her own instruction from the Prophet:

"The Prophet Joseph unbosomed his heart, and described the trying mental ordeal he experienced in overcoming the repugnance of his feelings, the natural result of the force of plural marriage. He knew the voice of God—he knew the commandment of the almighty to him was to go forward—to set the example, and establish Celestial plural marriage. He knew that he had not only his own prejudices and prepossessions to combat and to overcome, but those of the whole Christian world stared him in the face; but God, who is above all, had given the commandment, and He must be obeyed. Yet the Prophet hesitated and deferred from time to time, until an angel of God stood by him with a drawn sword, and told him that, unless he moved forward and established plural marriage, his Priesthood would be taken from him and he should be destroyed!"

In a similar manner Joseph approached Lorenzo. Eliza learned later that Joseph found a secluded spot on the bank of the Mississippi where he explained in detail to her brother the concept of Celestial Marriage. Actually, Lorenzo's mind had already been enlightened on the subject, so when he learned the full doctrine, he accepted it.

Eliza wrote later that that "Comforter which Jesus said should 'lead into all truth,' had penetrated his understanding, and while in England had given him an intimation of what at that time was, to many, a secret."

Lorenzo was convinced of the wisdom of plural marriage after listening to the Prophet. Up to that time he had not married, nor had he had any intentions of marrying. However, he was eager to accept counsel from the Prophet. According to Eliza, "It is one of his peculiarities to do nothing by halves." So Lorenzo had two wives sealed to him in the holy bonds of matrimony at the same time two years later.

A few days after his return from London, Lorenzo and Eliza traveled to Walnut Grove, 50 miles away, to visit their parents, who seemed comfortable in their newly settled community. Whether the parents knew of Eliza's marriage to the Prophet is not clear. However, we know that Eliza and Lorenzo were not the only Snows to enter plural marriage. Their sister Leonora had married Patriarch Isaac Morley as a plural wife and was living in Walnut Grove with him and the rest of his large family. It seems likely that the parents were aware of Eliza's marriage too, yet there is no evidence available that clearly indicates they knew.

The elder Snows were too exhausted from constant flight and persecution to endure much more. Their faith was being tested to the limit. Eliza, Lorenzo and Leonora knew their parents were slipping away from the church. It was a matter that Eliza took up in her journal: "The care and anxiety which I have experienced for the difficulties to which my parents have been subjected since our expulsion from our home in Mo. have been a source of much bitterness of feeling; and that bitterness has been aggravated by the reflection that they did not in their trials draw out from the springs of consolation which the gospel presents that support which was their privilege, and which would have enabled them to rejoice in the midst of tribulation and disappointment."

The senior Snows had had nearly all they could endure being Mormons. They were ready to leave the faith. This distressed Eliza, but it did not deter her own resolve to remain faithful.

By the close of 1843, conditions in Nauvoo had settled down somewhat. Though the Prophet was a hunted man, he commanded strength in the Nauvoo Legion under his leadership so that few outside authorities seeking to arrest him dared to do so.

Eliza, always surrounded by her friends and her faith, seemed not to feel the persecution to quite the same degree as many of the other women, especially Emma Smith. Somehow, Eliza found excitement and challenge in the constant confrontations. Her spirit, like a warrior's, soared with the thought that she would combat the forces of prejudice and intolerance, or at least personally support those who would do the fighting.

Despite persecution from the outside world, the consuming work and thought throughout the Nauvoo era concerned the erection of a temple, the second one to be built by the Saints. Plans were proceeding smoothly when Elias Higbee, one of the temple construction committee members, died suddenly on June 8, 1843. The community was filled with lamentation and wonder at the Lord taking one so vital to the construction of the temple.

Eliza wrote that Higbee's death "spread a feeling of deep sorrow over the City. It is a mysterious providence at this time, when every talent and exertion are peculiarly needed for the erection of Temple; that one of the Committee should be so suddenly call'd from time to eternity."

Not long after Higbee's death, events of mid-June, 1843, excited and troubled Eliza. Joseph, Emma and their children left for northern Illinois to visit Emma's relatives. Their departure proved timely for Joseph's safety. The governor of Missouri had issued a new writ for Joseph's arrest after someone had wounded former Governor Boggs with gunshot, nearly killing him. Naturally, the Prophet and his bodyguard, Porter Rockwell, were prime suspects in the case. The state of Illinois felt duty-bound at least to assist in the arrest of Joseph Smith.

A friend of Joseph's at the state capital, Judge James Adams, sent word to warn the Prophet of the impending arrest. Later the same day, the judge left Springfield for Nauvoo, arriving the following morning to assist the Prophet, still in the northern part of the state, any way he could.

On Sunday, June 25, 1843, the entire Mormon community— especially Eliza—was astir over the news that the Prophet had in fact been arrested.

"This afternoon," wrote Eliza, "while the people were assembled for service in the grove, Br. Clayton who had been sent with br. Markham to Lee Co. to notify Prest. Smith of the issue of the Writ for his arrest, returned which occasioned considerable excitement. He announced the capture of Prest. S. with his request that a number of the Militia should be sent to his assistance if needed. It was truly gratifying to see the spirit manifested on the occasion, not only by brethren but also by many persons not members of the church. All seem'd desirous of proving their patriotism in the cause of the persecuted prophet. The City literally swarmed with men who ran together from every quarter to volunteer their services. A selection of about eighty horsemen started about dusk, while fifty others were chosen to go by water, who went on board the 'Maid of Iowa' to go down the Mississippi and up the Illinois to Ottawa, expecting that Prest. S. would be taken there for trial."

Eliza must nearly have gone mad awaiting news, any news, of

the plight of the Prophet, her dearly loved husband.

The next day Emma arrived by buggy with her children. Eliza wrote, "I went to see her, and learned more particulars concerning the manner in which her husband was taken by H. Reynolds, Sheriff of Jackson Co. Mo. and Willson, a constable of Hancock Co. Ill. who came to Dixon on Rock river professing to be Mormon elders and enquired for Joseph Smith who they were informed was 12 miles distant at a place called Palestine Grove. They proceeded there and took him in a savage manner and brought him to Dixon, intending the same evening which was Friday the 23rd, to take him into Mo. but thro' the providential interference of the patriotic citizens of the place he was rescued and reserved for a more lawful proceeding."

Later that week Eliza learned that Joseph would soon be home. He came, triumphantly escorted into town by his two captors. The entire community of Nauvoo swarmed out to greet the Prophet while the Nauvoo Brass Band played martial music. Eliza described that joyous moment: "A military Escort accompanied by the Band and a number of ladies on horseback and a vast multitude of citizens, in carriages left the City at 11 o'clock A.M. and returned at 2, to the house of Prest. S. with the Prest. where I witness'd a scene of mingled joy and sorrow, which language cannot describe; for who can paint the emotions of the heart—the burst of parental and filial affection amid scenes of deepest anguish and the highest joy? The affectionate manner in which he introduced his family to those worse than savage officers."

Always the gracious host even though a prisoner, Joseph invited the arresting officers into his home for a feast with dozens of guests present. Joseph remained a prisoner until he was quickly taken before the municipal court of Nauvoo and acquitted.

Eliza, thrilled with the acquittal, rapturously struck off a 16-stanza ballad for the newspaper which she titled, "The Kidnapping of Lieutenant General Joseph Smith." It enjoyed popularity for a season. Years later, the ballad surfaced among historical documents that the church turned over to the energetic church historian, B.H. Roberts. Sorting through material to include in his mammoth work, *A Comprehensive History of the Church of Jesus Christ of Latter-day Saints*, Roberts rejected the ballad. He explained in a memo to then president of the church, Joseph F. Smith, why he did so: the Snow "poem," he said, added nothing "either of beauty or fact" to the account of Joseph Smith's arrest and release. "The verses," he insisted, "are the merest doggerel." Roberts concluded with his own brand of debunking Eliza's nineteenth-century verse: "All that jingles is not poetry."

But poetry was Eliza's favorite medium of self-expression. By no other means did she pour out her innermost thoughts so completely. B.H. Roberts' opinion notwithstanding, Eliza was considered a literary wonder by her contemporaries in Nauvoo.

Chapter Seven

Eliza had many opportunities to reflect on her life during the Nauvoo period, and it was from that time that some of her most enduring poetry comes. For the previous year and a half she had written, taught and socialized. She lived in two worlds—one as schoolteacher and poetess, the other as wife and zealot for her husband—the one very open, the other shrouded with secrecy and perhaps fear. Some of her poetry revealed this dual, sometimes divided, loyalty.

But there were many subjects she could openly write about. She praised the British queen in a poem to Queen Victoria, to whom Lorenzo had presented a specially bound copy of the *Book of Mormon* while he was in London. Hearing of her brother's act, Eliza wrote:

> Of all the monarchs of the earth,
> That wear the robes of royalty,
> She has inherited, by birth,
> The broadest wreath of majesty.

Specifically referring to her brother's presentation, Eliza penned this fifth stanza:

But, lo! a prize possessing more
Of worth than gems with honor rife—
A herald of salvation bore
To her the words of endless life.

Eliza also wrote many poems as letters or notes of encouragement to the sick, or as consolation to those bereaved at the loss of a loved one. In a comforting note to her good friend Mary Pratt, on the death of Mary's little son, Eliza gave the assurance that "all will be again restor'd." She concluded with this quatrain:

Altho' a tender branch is torn
Asunder from the parent tree;
Back to the trunk it shall be borne
And grafted for eternity.

She could lash out at those who had harmed her husband. In the *Wasp*, a Nauvoo paper that had but a short life, she wrote:

To Who Needs Consolation

O can a gen'rous spirit brook
With feelings of content
To see an age, distrustful look
On *thee* with *dark intent!*
I feel thy woes—my bosom shares
Thy spirit's agony:—
How can I love a heart that dares
Suspect thy purity?
I'll smile on all that smile on thee
As angels do above—
All who in pure sincerity
Will love thee, I will love.
Believe me, thou hast noble friends
Who feel and share thy grief;
And many a fervent pray'r ascends
To heav'n, for thy relief.

She also wrote of gaiety and love:

Conjugal
To Jonathan and Elvira

Like two streams, whose gentle forces
Mingling, in one current blend—

Like two waves, whose onward courses
To the ocean's bosom tend—

And so it went. Eliza's friends must have considered it an honor to have one of her poems written personally to them, because by the end of 1843 Eliza was being hailed as the "Poetess of Zion."

Eliza possessed, in the words of one historian, the "proud restraint of her New England ancestors," a restraint that cautioned her to reveal her inner self to few lest she be trampled on by the thoughtless.

It was her manner occasionally to seclude herself from the press of others, her teaching job notwithstanding. Eliza said herself that when she closed her day school for the year in March, 1843, after it had been open only three months, she did so "much to my *own* satisfaction..." She expressed perhaps her deepest feelings in a poem that touches the heart and allows the reader a small glimpse inside her. It is titled "Retirement":

> O how sweet is retirement! how precious these hours;
> They are dearer to me than midsummer's gay flowers
> Then soft stillness and silence awaken the Muse—
> 'Tis a time—'tis a place that minstrel should choose
> While so sweetly the moments in silence pass by
> When there's nobody here but Eliza and I.
>
> This is truly a moment peculiarly fraught
> With unbound meditation and freedom of thought!
> Such rich hallowed seasons are wont to inspire
> With the breath of Parnassus, the languishing lyre.
> For sweet silence is dancing in Solitude's eye
> When there's nobody here but Eliza and I.
>
> O thou fav'rite retirement! palladium of joys
> Remov'd from the bustle of nonsense and noise
> Where mind strengthens its empire—enlarges its sphere
> While it soars like the eagle or roams like the deer
> O these still, sober moments, how swiftly they fly
> While there's nobody here but Eliza and I.

In her own lifetime she was considered a master of arts. All of the small newspapers of the day solicited contributions of poetry, and none were more sought after than those of Eliza R. Snow. Many other poets regarded her as their mentor. Hannah Tapfield

King, a frequently published poetess in her own right, greatly admired Eliza. In a poem to her, Hannah wrote:

> My Spirit bends instinctively to thine;
> At thy feet I fain would sit and learn
> Like Paul of old before Gamaliel.

Others have not been so glowing in their evaluations. Maureen Ursenbach Beecher, an historian who has made a detailed study of Eliza's works, has criticized Eliza's art while giving the poetess full credit for teaching, chastising, encouraging and proselytizing through her lines. "Her collected poetry tells, better than do many prose accounts, the history of a faith in the building and a nation in the making. In her verses can be found the whole sweep of the Mormon story. But as poetry it fails of greatness. Twentieth century critics find it superficial, maudlin, trite and unimaginative."

In a comparison of Eliza's first valiant prize-winning efforts with later poems, Mrs. Beecher suggests that we may "assume she had slipped easily, effortlessly, into the popular style of her times. That is not to say the poetry is bad," the historian continued. "On the contrary, some of it reads quite well, and the suggestion made in a later biographical sketch that Eliza sacrificed a promising literary career to cast her lot with the Mormons may not be far from wrong." If such were the case, both Eliza and her peers considered the sacrifice justified.

Undoubtedly Eliza's single greatest contribution to the spirit of Zion, an anthem for the Saints, was her famous "Invocation," or "O My Father" as it became more popularly known:

> O my Father, thou that dwellest
> In the high and holy place;
> When shall I regain thy presence,
> And again behold thy face?

> In thy glorious habitation,
> Did my spirit once reside?
> In my first primeval childhood,
> Was I nurtur'd near thy side?

> For a wise and glorious purpose,
> Thou hast plac'd me here on earth;
> And withheld the recollection
> Of my former friends and birth;

Yet oft-times a secret something
Whisper'd, "You're a stranger here;"
And I felt that I had wander'd
From a more exalted sphere.

I had learned to call thee Father,
Through thy Spirit from on high;
But, until the Key of Knowledge
Was restor'd, I knew not why.

In the heavens are parents single?
No: the thought makes reason stare:
Truth is reason: truth eternal,
Tells me I've a mother there.

When I leave this frail existence—
When I lay this mortal by;
Father, Mother, may I meet you
In your royal court on high?

Then at length, when I've completed
All you sent me forth to do;
With your mutual approbation,
Let me come and dwell with you.

"O My Father" was penned at the height of the Nauvoo period, and it soon became the most widely sung congregational hymn in the church. More than just a simple expression of love for the Saints' Father in Heaven, "O My Father" was considered a revelation, especially so the line which states, "I've a mother there."

There are those who contend that Eliza got her concept of a "mother in heaven" from the Prophet Joseph. President Joseph F. Smith insisted in 1895 that God did not reveal His mind to a woman; therefore, he concluded, Eliza had learned the doctrine from the Prophet. On the other hand, just a few years prior to President Smith's remarks, Wilford Woodruff commented that Eliza had learned of the concept—which has since become "profound doctrine"—through revelation. Historical evidence indicates that Eliza learned of the doctrine through a close friend named Zina Huntington, whom the Prophet Joseph had comforted at the death of Zina's mother and who later became one of his plural wives. He had spoken of the Mother in Heaven doctrine "...in 1839, several years before the poem was first published. Zina would doubtless have confided such a revelation to her friend," Maureen Ursenbach Beecher has observed.

Another writer, Ellen Wallace, early speculated on the origin of Eliza's "O My Father," saying: "Constant association with the Prophet, intense love for the gospel and interest in the women's part led to many deep and earnest talks about the principles of salvation... The new light that the gospel turned on marriage [plural marriage] and motherhood glorified woman. What was her place in the final consummation of God's plan of salvation? Would she, Eliza Snow Smith, know her mother in the future life? Taking all these soul-stirring questions to the Prophet, she received from him the light and inspiration that resulted in the writing of the hymn 'O My Father.'"

The author went on to state, "So great was the inspiration burning within her, as she wrote that it did not leave her for days. And part of it entered the poem, for it has never been read even by the most casual reader without attracting attention."

David McKay, Sr., also wondered where Eliza got her inspiration, and he had an opportunity to ask her at the same time he questioned her about her marriage to Joseph. "Did the Lord reveal that doctrine of motherhood in heaven to you as He did to Rebekah when She was nearing the approach of Motherhood?" he asked. Eliza replied, "No indeed. When we were first organized as a Relief Society, the Prophet used to attend all our first meetings and gave us instructions in regards to our present duties and also taught many things that transpired in our Spirit home.... I got my inspiration from the Prophet's Teachings. All that I was required to do was to use my Poetical gift and give that Eternal principle in Poetry."

"O My Father" has caused a deep turn in traditional New World Christianity. The concept of a literal Mother in Heaven had no antecedent, except for the Roman influence of the Mother of Christ, in the Protestant world. It opened up a view of woman's role in the eternities—motherhood on a celestial level. The words express plainly the existence of a mother goddess residing in the highest realms of eternity at the side of a Heavenly Father. Understanding of the poem's lines has confirmed a greater, more exalted role for all women.

Orson F. Whitney, one of the outstanding authorities of the church at the turn of the century, wrote of Eliza's creation: "If all her other writings, prose and verse, were swept into oblivion, this poem alone, the sweetest and sublimest of all the songs of Zion, would perpetuate her fame and render her name immortal." He was prophetic in his utterance, for that is nearly what has happened in the twentieth century.

Through the years, "O My Father" has justly been labeled "the proselytizing hymn." It has been sung in all areas of the globe and in most tongues, carrying with its message a strong conviction of the Mormon praise of Father and Mother in Heaven.

In the latter part of the nineteenth century, a popular anecdote circulated among the Mormons about Eliza's influence on a popular evangelist, Theodore Parker: "It is said that the celebrated Evangelist of America, Theodore Parker, had in his service a Mormon woman; that he had known nothing of her connection with the Mormon Church; that this female disciple of the Mormon Prophet, in a spirit of praiseworthy cunning to captivate her master's mind with the striking conceptions of her church on the subect of pre-existence, placed a little book of Eliza R. Snow's poems near his hand; that Theodore Parker read the hymn 'O My Father,' was captivated with its conceptions of our Father and Mother God and their courts on high; that he talked to his servant of this hymn and the Mormons; and that Eliza R. Snow's hymn gave the inspiration to the unique form of invocation 'to our Father and Mother God' which characterized Theodore Parker's adorations and prayers."

"O My Father," according to one authority, "is much sung, not for its literary but for its theological content."

Whatever the literary merits of Eliza's poetry and prose, the fact remains that she inspired an entire community of Saints, both in and about Nauvoo and as they later traveled west, giving them the most valuable support those discouraged people could receive from among their group—courage.

Chapter Eight

Christmas festivities, with their underlying message of peace, invited even the persecuted to set aside their anxieties for a brief season. Eliza and her brother, Lorenzo, traveled to the Morley settlement in Lima to celebrate New Year's Eve, 1843, with their sister, Leonora. Wrote Eliza, "A social circle of a few choice friends convened at the house of our sister [Leonora], and we had a lovely time." An insight into the type of celebration they held came from Eliza, who very formally stated that she acted as "secretary pro tem" for the gathering. After it occurred to her that the group should hear from Lorenzo, "I made the motion, which was seconded and carried unanimously (of course); and responding, he gave a very interesting address—beautifully adapted to the occasion and to the peculiar circumstances of those present."

Eliza wrote several poems reflecting on the evening and more generally on the year just past. She penned "Psalms Second," dealing with the tribulations of the Saints and blessings from the Lord, and also a work she titled "The Past Year," a piece of blank verse dealing with time and visions.

Eliza's works at that point dealt optimistically with the future of the Saints. It was as if she felt the persecutions were behind them: "He hath rolled back the waves of persecution—He hath staid [sic] the hour of oppression—He hath brought their names into derision, who dealt out to us the cup of affliction."

Lorenzo was not so easily convinced that the Saints' enemies would not heap yet more trouble onto the Mormons' weary shoulders. He said in that evening's address that the members perhaps "shall then meet other things of an unpleasant nature."

Eliza spent much of her time at the Morley settlement in Lima for the first four months of 1844, but then she moved back to Nauvoo. On one of her visits in April when she had gone to the city to attend conference, she had visited with the splendid Col. Stephen Markham and his family, and they had invited her to live with them in Nauvoo. Of all the families Eliza lived with, the Markhams would host her over the longest period of time.

Stephen, a "well-to-do farmer" when he joined the church in Ohio, was faithful to the church to the end of his life. A former military man with solid finances, the able colonel was one to whom the Prophet turned time and again for assistance.

The Markhams had moved into their new log house just weeks prior to Eliza's visit. During the height of the Prophet's series of legal battles to save himself from being returned to Missouri, Stephen Markham had sold his fine large house in Nauvoo for $1,200 and had given all the money to Joseph. For over a year the Markhams had lived in a tent. Next to members of the Smith family, there was no one any more loyal to the Prophet than Stephen Markham whom Joseph trusted.

Eliza seemed eager to move in with the Markhams. Undoubtedly she felt she could not live again with the Smiths, even though they were residing in the newly constructed Nauvoo House, which afforded ample space for Eliza had she been welcome. But surely the strain on the Smiths and her as well would have been too great.

At the time she moved in with the Markhams, Eliza apparently had no independent source of income or any assets of her own, except the luggage and clothing she carried. It is possible that she had never retrieved the loss of her property in Kirtland. Her father had lost his holdings there and again in Adam-Ondi-Ahman. Even later in Walnut Grove, his farm was stormed and he was again driven out. Eliza was dependent on others for support, though she was always willing to tutor, clean, sew or perform a host of other tasks for her keep.

Little is available about Eliza's life for the next two years. Strangely, the remainder of the entries in her Nauvoo journal are poetry, yet for Eliza as well as others, the months that followed that April conference held perhaps the greatest personal sorrow she and others would be forced to endure.

The Prophet had just declared himself a candidate for President of the United States. He had decided that others seemed ill fit for the job, and that he could garner political strength for his people by running for office. That act, along with rumors of spiritual wifery, created resentment throughout the state of Illinois similar to the ill will which had developed in Missouri just five years earlier. Illinois wanted to curtail the Mormons in their political efforts, so state officials decided to revoke the Nauvoo city charter through a legislative decree. The Mormons resisted.

Elements of anti-Mormonism swelled within the city itself. When Joseph Smith, as mayor of Nauvoo, ordered destruction of the printing press of the *Nauvoo Expositor*, all hell broke loose. That single act inflamed the region, provoking the governor of Illinois to declare martial law in the city of Nauvoo and subsequently the arrest of Joseph Smith. The Prophet was taken to the county jail in Carthage, a day's ride from Nauvoo, and imprisoned there.

It was late in June, 1844, at the county jail that a mob, their faces smeared with mud mixed with gunpowder for a disguise, stormed the stone prison and shot to death Joseph and his brother, Hyrum.

When Eliza was told of the Prophet's murder, at first she refused to believe it. He had already escaped from countless life-threatening situations. Why not now?

When at last she was convinced of the terrible truth, she was devastated with grief. No doubt it was especially hard for Eliza to suffer the death of her husband, because she was unable to express her feelings as a wife. Restraining her most personal, tender thoughts, Eliza's only recorded reactions seem those of a spokesperson for the church rather than those of a heartbroken widow.

Even years later when she had the opportunity to enlighten

historians as to her deepest thoughts and actions at that tragic time, she did not. In a biography of her brother which Eliza compiled in 1884—a work that was, in fact, as much an account of her own life—Eliza chose to include her brother's journal entry of the martyrdom rather than express her own observations and feelings. When she pieced together fragments of her life for compiler Hubert Howe Bancroft in the 1870s, she fiercely chided both the national and the Illinois public officials more in essay form than personal reflection. She wrote these terse words of reproach and condemnation: "The awful tragedy of the 27th of June 1844, is a livid, burning, scathing stain on our national escutcheon. To look upon the noble, lifeless forms of those brothers, Joseph and Hyrum Smith, lying side by side, after having been brought home from Carthage, where they had been slaughtered in their manhood and in their innocence, was a sight that might well appal [sic] the heart of a true American citizen: but what it was for loving wives and children, the loyal heart may feel, but let language keep silence.

"This scene occurred in America, 'The land of the free, and home of the brave,' to which our ancestors fled for religious freedom...."

On and on she wrote, but as she did she allowed the opportunity to share her personal insights into that scene slip from recorded history.

Characteristically, Eliza's poems, written for public dissemination, may have been her consolation. In a work published in the local newspaper four days after the assassination, the poetess expressed her tribute to the martyred brothers:

THE ASSASSINATION
OF GENERALS JOSEPH SMITH AND HYRUM SMITH,

First Presidents Of The Church Of Jesus Christ Of Latter-Day Saints, Who Were Massacred By A Mob, In Carthage, Hancock Co., Ill., On The 27th Of June, 1844.

And when he had opened the fifth seal, I saw under the altar the souls of them that were slain for the word of God, and for the testimony which they held:

And they cried with a loud voice, saying, How long, O Lord, holy and true, doest thou not judge and avenge our blood on them that dwell on the earth?

And white robes were given unto every one of them; and it was said unto them, that they should rest yet for a little season, until their fellow servants also and their brethren, that should be killed as they were, should be fulfilled.

Rev., vi, 9, 19, 11.

Ye heavens, attend! Let all the earth give ear!
Let Gods and seraphs, men and angels hear:
The worlds on high—the universe shall know,
What awful scenes are acted here below!
Had Nature's self a heart, her heart would bleed
At the recital of so foul a deed;
For never, since the Son of God was slain,
Has blood so noble flowed from human vein,
As that which now on God for vengeance calls
From "Freedom's" ground—from Carthage prison walls.

Oh, Illinois! thy soil has drunk the blood
Of Prophets, martyred for the truth of God
Once loved America! what can atone
For the pure blood of innocence thou'st sown?
Were all thy streams in teary torrents shed,
To mourn the fate of those illustrious dead,
How vain the tribute for the noblest worth,
That graced thy surface, O degraded earth!

Vile, wretched murderers, fierce for human blood,
You've slain the Prophets of the living God;
Who've borne oppression from their early youth,
To plant on earth, the principles of truth.
Shades of our patriot fathers! Can it be,
Beneath your blood-stained flag of liberty,
The firm supporters of our country's cause,
Are butchered while submissive to her laws?
Yes, blameless men, defamed by hellish lies,
Have thus been offered as a sacrifice,
T'appease the ragings of a brutish clan,
That has defied the laws of God and man!
'Twas not for crime or guilt of theirs, they fell:
Against the laws they never did rebel.
True to their country, yet her plighted faith
Has proved an instrument of cruel death.

Great men have fallen, mighty men have died—
Nations have mourned their fav'rites and their pride;

But, two so wise, so virtuous and so good,
Before on earth, at once have never stood
Since the creation—men whom God ordained,
To publish truth where error long had reigned;
Of whom the world itself unworthy proved;
It *knew them not*, but men with hatred moved,
And with infernal spirits have combined
Against the best—the noblest of mankind.

O, persecution! shall thy purple hand
Spread utter desolation through the land?
Shall freedom's banner be no more unfurled?
Has peace, indeed, been taken from the world?
Thou God of Jacob, in this trying hour,
Help us to trust in Thy Almighty power—
Support the Saints beneath this awful stroke—
Make bare Thine arm to break oppression's yoke.
We mourn Thy Prophet, from whose lips have flowed
The words of life Thy Spirit has bestowed—
A depth of thought no human art could reach,
From time to time flowed in sublimest speech,
From Thy celestial fountain, through his mind,
To purify and elevate mankind;
The rich intelligence by him brought forth,
Is like the sunbeam spreading o'er the earth.

Now Zion mourns—she mourns an earthly head;
Her Prophet and her Patriarch are dead;
The blackest deed that men and devils know,
Since Calv'rys scene, has laid the brothers low.
One while in life, and *one* in death—they proved
How strong their friendship—how they truly loved;
True to their mission, until death they stood,
Then sealed their testimony with their blood.

All hearts with sorrow bleed, and every eye
Is bathed in tears; each bosom heaves a sigh;
Heart broken widows' agonizing groans
Are mingled with the helpless orphans' moans.
Ye saints! be still, and know that God is just—
With steadfast purpose in His promise trust;
Girded with sackcloth, own His mighty hand,
And wait His judgments on this guilty land.
The noble Martyrs now have gone to move
The cause of Zion in the courts above.

A month later Eliza published in the Nauvoo newspaper, *Times and Seasons*, a mighty tribute to Joseph in a poem titled, "Praise to the Man." The poem has since been sung by countless thousands of Mormons in meetings across the world to the tune of "Star In The East." Eliza wrote:

Praise to the man who communed with Jehovah!
Jesus anointed that "Prophet and Seer"—
Blessed to open the last dispensation;
Kings shall extol him and nations revere.

Praise to his mem'ry, he died as a martyr,
Honored and blessed be his ever great name!
Long shall his blood which was shed by assassins,
Stain Illinois while the earth lauds his fame.

Great is his glory, and endless his Priesthood,
Ever and Ever the keys he will hold,
Faithful and true he will enter his kingdom,
Crowned in the midst of the Prophets of old.

Sacrifice brings forth the blessings of heaven;
Earth must atone for the blood of that man;
Wake up the world for the conflict of justice;
Millions shall know "brother Joseph" again.

Chorus
Hail to the Prophet, ascended to heaven!
Traitors and tyrants now fight him in vain;
Mingling with Gods he can plan for his brethern [sic];
Death cannot conquer that hero again.

Not surprisingly, the lines:

"Long shall his blood which was shed by assassins
Stain Illinois while the earth lauds his fame"

have, through the years, been softened to read:

"Long shall his blood which was shed by assassins
Plead unto heaven while the earth lauds his fame."

Also of interest is the fact that in the present-day hymnbook of the Church of Jesus Christ of Latter-day Saints, William W. Phelps, Eliza's contemporary and fellow poet, is given credit for "Praise to the Man." There can be little doubt, however, that Eliza is the true author. In the *Times and Seasons* issue of August 1, 1844, Eliza's name is ascribed to the poem. And in December, 1849, the

Frontier Guardian of Kanesville, Iowa, introduced the poem as follows: "Lines written by Miss Eliza R. Snow, upon the martyrdom of Joseph Smith, the Prophet and Seer." Certainly the current credit given to W.W. Phelps can be no more than a printer's error. The very soul of the words are Eliza's as surely as "O My Father" belongs to her skilled pen.

Much later, in the seclusion of the Rocky Mountains, Eliza reflected that she had often wondered whether Jesus could know anything about the pains of women. At last she decided "that God in order to be God, must know the suffering of woman as well as man."

Surely Eliza realized that God knew of her pain. Widowed, childless and so in need of the strength of a man, she must have suffered deeply.

Eliza—An Emerging Leader

Chapter Nine

From his position in the front seat of his fine two-seater buggy, Stephen Markham reined in his horses at Sugar Creek, on the Iowa side of the Mississippi. Eliza, Hannah Markham and one of the Markhams' sons sat in the rear. The cold daylight of February 13th, 1846, revealed a field of tents and scattered wagons. As she scanned the scene, it appeared to Eliza to be an entire city of tents.

Once again the Mormons were tramping into exile. This time, as in Missouri eight years before, Eliza and others were fleeing their homes to escape mob violence that had reached fever pitch. But now they were leaving behind their beautiful city, Nauvoo.

Eliza and the Markhams were among the late travelers in the first wave of cold, resolute refugees heading west. The campsite called Sugar Creek had been designated the meeting place of the fleeing Saints. There they would wait in comparative safety until all who intended to go west had settled their business affairs, gathered their supplies and extricated themselves from the dangers in Nauvoo. Their leaders had for months been urging them to prepare, but many had procrastinated, reluctant to leave their comfortable homes. Finally, conditions had become so frightening that the command was given to pick up and leave. Those who were ill-prepared fled with the others to Sugar Creek and then, with the assistance of their more prudent brethren, readied themselves for the long journey as best they could.

Later that first day, Eliza and company found her brother, Lorenzo, camped with his wives and children. Alongside was the Yearsley family, friends who invited them in to spend the night.

By breakfast time the next morning, all the tents were buried beneath a fresh sheet of snow. Eliza worked her way out from the tent and into the Markham buggy, which offered a measure of protection with its enclosed fringed top. There she remained, according to Eliza, "and did not leave it till the next day. Sis. M [Markham] and I did some needlework tho' the melting snow dripped thro' our cover."

It had been a year and eight months since the death of the Prophet. In that turbulent time, Eliza had remained at the Markham home and involved herself in temple activities. She had helped to make clothing and blankets for the temple builders, and finally she was called by Brigham Young to enter the temple and replace Emma Smith as the "high priestess" of the women. There she received authority to perform the special temple ordinances. Not only did she preside over the sisters, but she was also the official recorder in the temple.

Just prior to leaving Nauvoo, Eliza—as well as a number of Joseph's other plural wives—was married, for this life only, to the new prophet and leader of the church, Brigham Young. Of that marriage and all its implications, little is recorded. We know from statements of friends and family that Brigham Young usually called Eliza Sister Snow and that she addressed him as President Young. From the start the marriage was an arrangement that best suited them both. Brigham Young provided a comfortable home for Eliza and financed all her needs, while she in turn became his liaison with the female portion of the church. As one of twenty-seven wives, Eliza would become his respected counselor and confidante. Why not a consummated marriage? The record does not say. Certainly Eliza's love and affection had been for Joseph. But if Joseph was the "crown of her life," then Brigham was the steward of her mortal destiny.

Conditions in Nauvoo during January and early February,

1846, with the governor of Illinois demanding that the Mormons leave, were too chaotic to permit much semblance of a broad family unity. For the following two years, the hectic pace would prohibit Brigham Young from providing for any but the most immediate needs of his now larger family. However, with his keen, orderly mind and his ability to organize, Brigham made arrangements for each of his wives and their children to be transported across the plains to the valleys of Utah. It was he who arranged with Stephen Markham for Eliza's safe conduct and provisions. Eliza, quite accustomed to fending for herself, would manage and even excel in the role of pioneer. Not encumbered by children, her leadership talents soon began to surface, so that throughout the weeks of exodus to a temporary encampment, sisters up and down the trail from Nauvoo to Winter Quarters would look to her for compassionate service.

Eliza referred to their destination as the "Western wilderness." The exact location of the area where Brigham Young was leading them was not widely known when the Saints crossed the river from Nauvoo, heading into a sparsely settled area of Iowa. Some speculated on California, along the Pacific Coast. As a matter of fact, one shipload of Saints left by water to go around the Horn to Yorba Buena in northern California. Some more accurately speculated that the Saints would end up somewhere in the Rocky Mountains. It seems plausible that Eliza spoke with Brigham Young on the matter, though there is no indication that she did in the compact journal she kept.

On the western shores of the Mississippi, Eliza witnessed for herself the trauma of that mid-winter flight. Of that experience she later wrote: "We had been preceded by thousands, and I was informed that on the first night of the encampment nine children were born into the world, and from that time, as we journeyed onward, mothers gave birth to off-spring under almost every variety of circumstances imaginable, except those to which they had been accustomed; some in tents, others in wagons—in rainstorms and in snow-storms. I heard of one birth which occurred under the rude shelter of a hut, the sides of which were formed of blankets fastened to poles stuck in the ground, with a bark roof through which the rain was dripping. Kind sisters stood holding dishes to catch the water as it fell, thus protecting the new-comer and its mother from a shower-bath as the little innocent first entered on the stage of human life; and through faith in the great ruler of events, no harm resulted to either."

Eliza was quick to point out to the casual reader that those women out on Sugar Creek in the slush of winter were not "savages, accustomed to roam the forest and brave the storm and tempest ... most of them were born and educated in the Eastern States."

In her recollection of those trying days Eliza went on to note: "From the 13th to the 18th we had several snow-storms and very freezing weather, which bridged the Mississippi sufficiently for crossing heavily loaded wagons on the ice. We were on timbered land, had plenty of wood for fuel, and the men rolled heavy logs together, and kept large fires burning around the bright blaze of which, when not necessarily otherwise engaged, they warmed themselves. The women, when the duties of cooking and its et ceteras did not prompt them out, huddled with their children into wagons and carriages for protection from the chilling breeze."

Within a three-week period, a vast wagon train moved out of Sugar Creek and began its long, painful journey west. The Mormons' prime objectives were to create distance between themselves and the Illinois mob that had plundered and driven them literally into the snow-covered wilderness, and to find an isolated land where they could live in peace.

Usually wagon trains pulled by mules or oxen covered about five miles a day. On Saturday, February 28, they again encountered snowy weather. "We travelled but 4 miles," Eliza recorded, "and encamped in a low, truly romantic valley just large enough for our tents, wagons, etc. We arrived a little before sunset and the prospect for the night seemed dubious enough. The ground was covered with snow, shoe deep but our industrious men with hoes soon prepared places and pitched the tents, built wood-piles in front of them, and but a few minutes with many hands transformed the rude valley into a thriving town on Indian creek."

No matter how much Eliza and other recorders of those bleak days of winter on the march recalled the hardships, in reality there were also special moments and high spirits. When the Twelve Apostles arrived at Indian Creek accompanied by the ever popular Nauvoo Brass Band, the members felt they were part of something exciting and vital to the development of the church.

Undaunted as always, Eliza wrote several rousing pioneer songs, among them "The Camp of Israel."

Lo! a num'rous host of people
Tented on the western shore
Of the noble Mississippi
They for weeks were crossing o'er.
At the last day's dawn of winter,
Bound with frost and wrapt in snow.
Hark! the sound is onward, onward!
Camp of Israel! rise and go.

All at once is life in motion
Trunks and beds and baggage fly:
Oxen yok'd and horses harness'd
Tents roll'd up, are passing by.
Soon the carriage wheels are rolling
Onward to a woodland dell,
Where at sunset all are quarter'd—
Camp of Israel! All is well.

Thickly round, the tents are cluster'd
Neighb'ring smokers together blend—
Supper served—the hymns are chanted
And the evening pray'rs ascend.
Last of all the guards are station'd—
Heavens! Must guards be serving here?
Who would harm the houseless exiles?
Camp of Israel! Never fear.

Where is freedom? Where is justice?
Both have from this nation fled;
And the blood of martyr'd Prophets,
Must be answer'd on its head!
Therefore to your tents, O Jacob!
Like our Father Abr'm dwell!—
God will execute his purpose—
Camp of Israel! All is well.

The first leg of the trip west was, for Eliza, generally seen from inside a covered buggy. "My dormitory, sitting-room, writing-office and frequently dining room, was the buggy in which Sister Markham, her little son David, and I, rode. One of my brother's wives had one of the old-fashioned foot-stoves, which proved very useful. She frequently brought it to me, filled with live coals from one of those mammoth fires—a kindness which I remember with gratitude; but withal, I frosted my feet enough to occasion inconvenience for weeks afterwards."

Before Eliza, her brother Lorenzo and sister Leonora left Illinois, they had made one last, fruitless trip to try and persuade their parents to dispose of their lands and trudge west. Oliver and Rosetta Snow refused. They were elderly and exhausted from trying to remain Mormons under the pressure of so much persecution. The three Snow children had already determined to follow the church movement. They bid farewell, sadly. Eliza would never see her parents again.

Evenings, though cold and wintry, must have been personally stimulating for Eliza. With no children to care for and the supper over, Eliza began her evening visits to encourage the sisters.

Literally thousands of Mormons were slushing their way across Iowa that spring. So large were the encampments that the leaders found it necessary to break up the Saints into groups of what they called "Companies of Fifty." Throughout late February and early March, latecomers from Nauvoo and surrounding communities drifted into the expanding camps. It was much like a traveling city. Eliza, at least, thought so, and many others saw a resemblance to the children of Israel as they journeyed in the wilderness.

One evening Eliza and Hannah Markham left their tent to stroll through the camp calling on various people. They stopped at Amasa Lyman's tent to chat, but the two friendly visitors soon realized that without assistance they would likely not find their way back to their own tent. Eliza expressed as much when she wrote, "After a little chat with them Bro. Lyman conducted us toward home until we came in sight of it, which we could hardly have found without a pilot."

By March 4, Stephen Markham had traded his fine buggy for a "lumber wagon." Now as they journeyed, Eliza noted that they were riding slowly through the countryside "nicely seated in an ox wagon, on a chest with a brass kettle and the soap box for our footstools, thankful that we are as well off."

The trek was difficult, especially crossing marshes, rivers and creeks. Eliza wrote: "After crossing the river the road was thro' timber and intolerably muddy, the banks on this side rising almost perpendicularly. The teams had hard work to draw the loads as we ascended hill after hill.... Left the timber-road, very bad for a mile or more—the weather warm and the ox-teams seemed almost exhausted. I got out of the wagon and walk'd for the first time on the journey ... arrived at the place of our encampment after dark, tho' not in the dark for the moon shone brilliantly upon our path. 10 or 12 miles this day."

Always, they rested over Sunday, sometimes deciding to remain camped a day or two longer. It is interesting to note how quickly the pioneers got the camp set up and in a matter of hours had a city in operation, no doubt due to the skill of their leaders: "Our town yesterday morning has grown to a 'City,' laid out in the form of a half hollow square, fronting east and south, on a beautiful level, with an almost perpendicular on one side and on the other, a gradual descent to a deep ravine on the west and north. At nine this morning I noticed, but a few rods from our tent, a blacksmith's shop in operation, and everything indicated real life. Not a cooking utensil was idle. Sister M [Markham] baked a batch of eleven loaves but the washing business was necessarily omitted for the want of water, an inconvenience the present location suffers more than any previous one."

On Monday, March 9, 1846, Brigham Young stopped at Eliza's company. Of that visit she mentioned that she had "the pleasure of the first interview with Pres. Young since we left the City." By "City," she meant Nauvoo.

Solicitous of her though the Markhams were, it was not easy for Eliza to travel with them. As the journey lengthened, the Markhams' patience with one another shortened. The two quarreled frequently, causing Eliza to feel uncomfortably trapped in the middle of their disputes. She complained in her diary: "This morning a circumstance occur'd which renew'd my reflections on the subject of family government. Without order all is confusion, and without mutual action in the head, (and mutual feeling and mutual understanding must produce mutual action) there can be no order. One parent must support the claims to respect for the other and this can never be done while either exposes the faults of the other in the presence of the children."

Hannah Markham, who felt she had endured nearly all she could, kept up a stream of complaints against her husband. At one point after an argument, Col. Markham moved his wagon "some 40 or 50 rods to a creek," separating from his wife and family, as well as Eliza, an action clearly a blessing to Eliza's ears.

Though Hannah and Stephen Markham managed to finish the long journey together, in a few years Hannah would leave her husband and take her sons on to California, so bitter would become the family fights.

Often there were small favors shown among the sisters on the trail. Eliza sent items she knitted or sewed to various friends, and in return they would send her a small treat, usually food: "Catherine sent us some nice sweet biscuits. . . . Sister Y [Young] sent us a supper of rich pot-pie made of wild game, rabbits, pheasants, quail, and c., which is the fourth dish of the kind on which we have feasted since we left the city being four weeks yesterday."

Whenever the wind blew strong and cold, Eliza lashed out at those who had driven them from Nauvoo. March 15 was so cold and windy that the tents blew down and the women huddled all day in the wagon. "The subject of 'brotherly oppression' was forcibly presented to my view," Eliza wrote in her anger, "and I was led to inquire 'How long O Lord?' Is there no reward for patient submission? Will the insolent oppressor always go unpunished? How long shall some feast, while others famish?"

Deep was Eliza's resentment of the Illinois persecutors who had driven the Mormons from their fine farms and stately brick houses in Nauvoo.

But the Saints were not starving. On the contrary, Brigham Young had organized the entire exodus to the west with the skill of a general in full command. He had divided the total migrating mass of pioneers into groups of 600 which were further separated into smaller families of 50 and 10. There were presidents and captains over each 50, and captains over each 10. One of the quasi-military aspects of the trek centered around supplies. Brigham Young and his leaders had allowed for one traveling commissary, a supply store on wheels, for each hundred persons in the camp.

The rigorous study and military discipline that the Prophet Joseph had drilled into most of the leaders paid off handsomely as the entire body of the church moved across the plains of Iowa. Eliza noted how very strict "President Young" was when she wrote, "Bishop Miller and the Pratts who are encamped some miles ahead, are recalled to attend a court and answer to the charge of disregarding council, and c." Kindly prophet though he may have been, Brigham tolerated no dissent, nor disobedience to his law. Eliza admired the iron-willed attitude of "President Young"; she was made very much of the same ingredients.

Though no one starved, supplies were meager, and sometimes food had to be rationed. The horses and oxen required a great deal of grain. But there were towns along the route of the camp. At times companies of men either volunteered or were commanded to leave and get jobs with local farmers. The Nauvoo Brass Band offered to play at festivities in the vicinity of the camp. Whole communities enjoyed the martial music and paid for the entertainment. Men who found work on neighboring farms generally were paid in foods—apples, dried fruits, meat, corn, whatever the local farmers had to give. All commodities were received with thanksgiving.

Eliza referred with bitterness to one of the many towns they journeyed through: "As we passed through a town on the Des Moines river, the inhabitants manifested as much curiosity as though they were viewing a traveling menagerie of wild animals. Their levity and apparent heartlessness was, to me, proof of profound ignorance. How little did those people comprehend our movement, and the results the Almighty had in view."

The Saints had been traveling for two months when instructions came from Brigham Young that each company of 10 was to meet together and partake of the sacrament. Eliza noted that they "attended to the ordinance for the first time since we left the 'City.'" Joyously she continued, "My heart was made to rejoice in the privilege of once more commemorating the death of Him whom I desire to behold. Roll on ye wheels of time! Hasten, thou long anticipated period, when He shall again stand upon the earth."

The journey seemed especially hard for Eliza as she watched the draft animals suffer without sufficient food: "We were in the season significantly termed 'between hay and grass' and the teams, feeding mostly on browse, wasted in flesh, and had but little strength; and it was painful, at times, to see the poor creatures straining every joint and ligature, doing their utmost, and looking the very picture of discouragement."

She explained further how the rain-soaked ground stalled the heavy wagons, requiring the doubling of teams to move each wagon. Life on the prairie that spring was perhaps even harder for the women with children. Eliza noted that "many of our sisters walked all day, rain or shine, and at night prepared suppers for their families, with no sheltering tents; and then made their beds in and under wagons that contained their earthly all. How frequently, with intense sympathy and admiration, I watched the mother, when, forgetful of her own fatigue and destitution, she took unwearied pains to fix up, in the most palatable form, the allotted portion of food...."

Little had Eliza realized when she left Nauvoo how varied her experiences would be before she reached her destination. As Eliza's division of Saints neared one of their semi-permanent settlements, Mt. Pisgah, in Iowa, she recorded that "requisitions came officially to President Young, from the United States Government, demanding five hundred efficient men to be drawn from our traveling camps, to enter the United States military service, and march immediately to California and assist in the war with Mexico."

Regardless of their misgivings toward "an unprotective government, under which they had been exiled from their homes," volunteers immediately answered the call on horseback, gathering others all along their wagon trail until in an incredibly short time they had the 500 men who constituted the famed Mormon Battalion. Though loyal to their country, patriotism was not their only motive. Brigham Young had struck a bargain with government agents. The wages earned by the men of the battalion, above those funds needed for individual sustenance, were to be sent to him to provide much-needed-supplies for the members of his migrating church.

Eliza felt pride in the volunteers' willing response, yet she was clearly aware of the hardships the remaining travelers would face. "But it was a heavy tax—a cruel draft," she wrote later, "—one which imposed accumulated burdens on those who remained, especially our women, who were under the necessity of driving their own teams from the several points from which their husbands and sons left, to the Salt Lake Valley."

Thus the job of driving their own team of oxen fell to Eliza and Hannah Markham. However, because Hannah and others of the Markham group soon became ill with the ague, an illness of chills and fever which swept through Mt. Pisgah, Eliza's only recourse was to drive the oxen single-handedly the remainder of the distance to Winter Quarters, which amounted to a 12-day journey.

Eliza described her experience: "Had it been a horse-team I should have been amply qualified, but driving oxen was entirely a new business; however, I took the whip and very soon learned to 'haw and gee,' and acquitted myself, as teamster, quite honorably, driving most of the way to winter quarters. The cattle were so well trained that I could sit and drive. At best, however, it was fatiguing—the family being all sick by turns, and at times I had to cook, as well as nurse the sick; all of which I was thankful for strength to perform."

Eliza may have been thankful for strength, but shortly after her company arrived at Winter Quarters she too came down with the chills and fever she undoubtedly contracted from the others. It was the worst illness Eliza experienced in her life: "I was taken sick on the last day of August of a fever, which ran nearly 40 days and terminated in the chills and fever. During this time, while suffering much in body, and lying as it were at the gate of death, with family discord [the Markhams' ongoing feud with each other] which I think proper to call 'hell,' reigning around me, I had the satisfaction of experiencing kindness from many of my friends ... without whose attention I must have suffer'd much more, as I was the last in the family taken sick and nobody able to wait on or administer to me as I needed. I cannot recollect dates, but not long after the commencement of my sickness a heavy rain came on and the bed where I lay was wet almost from head to foot, but the Lord preserv'd my life, and while I live I will speak of His goodness."

Indeed, the Lord had preserved the life of Eliza R. Snow. Still ahead, there were many great works for her to perform.

Chapter Ten

Just across the Missouri River from Council Bluffs, the migrating Saints halted for a season, not daring to risk pulling their heavy wagons over the steep passes of the Rocky Mountains in the dead of winter. In the late fall of 1846, about 4,000 Mormons hurriedly constructed the best shelters they could contrive to protect themselves from the Nebraska storms. They built about 600 log houses, 85 more made of sod, and others were merely dugouts in hillsides. Some even lived in wagons throughout the winter.

At first, however, before the rude huts could be constructed, the Saints were exposed to the harsh elements of nature, aggravating the illnesses so prevalent among their number. For Eliza, the exposure proved nearly fatal.

Helen Mar Whitney, wife of Newel K. Whitney, wrote, "I never knew Sister Eliza intimately until we arrived at Winter Quarters. There I made her acquaintance under peculiar and trying circumstances. She was lying sick with a fever in a poorly covered wagon, with the blazing sun beating down upon it. Many more were in a similar condition and had no other shelter, until after the heavy rains were on us and the nights had become cold and frosty, but in the midst of these trials, with trusting faith in the Almighty, the Saints were sustained and comforted."

Eliza suffered through most of the chilly fall bedded down in a makeshift dugout of logs and mud. But when a measure of health came back to her, she was up and moving around camp. It had never been her nature to let others serve her when she had strength to care for herself.

According to Helen Mar Whitney, "Eliza was able to go around and administer to her sisters in affliction: she comforted those who stood in need. Her words dropped like refreshing dew from the heavens, like manna, when most needed, reviving and giving new hope to the weary and hungry."

Early on at Winter Quarters, the Markhams parted company, saving Eliza from the torment of constant bickering between the husband and wife. She made note of the separation when she wrote, "Without attempting to describe the cause, one night, probably after many of the Camp had retired ... a conversation took place between Col. Markham and his wife of a most disgraceful nature; and the loud and fervent tones in which it was uttered must have made it quite public thro'out the Camp. Revenge and retaliation seem'd the ruling spirits of each, and the pow'rs of darkness seem'd holding a jubilee around us."

Shortly after that scene Eliza found herself thrust into the very center of their battle, much to her consternation. It seems that not only were the Markham parents at odds, but the children were prone to quarrel as well. During a heated discussion with his father, Warren Markham insinuated that Eliza had been speaking to Elder Heber C. Kimball, their division leader, against Warren's wife. He did not name Eliza personally, but identified her as "one that we have been supporting all the while, and one in the family."

An outraged Eliza took up her pen and vented her feelings in her diary. For a person given to vague entries fraught with hidden meanings, her record of that painful experience is uncharacteristically detailed and emotional.

"Is such the grateful return which I am to receive for sharing the disgrace, and for all my exertions in upholding the reputation of this unfortunate family?" she wrote. "They are and have been as kind to me as their circumstances would admit; but the Lord knows I have done them more good than all the trouble I have made them, be it ever so much.

"I am reminded of the feelings of Job when he exclaimed, 'Young men have risen up against me whose fathers I would have disdain'd to *have set with the dogs of my flock.*'"

Eliza's journal indicates an ongoing dispute with the Markhams which lasted several days, but finally Eliza, true to her finest qualities, set aside her disagreements and acknowledged her appreciation for their kindnesses to her.

Those kindnesses continued, for Stephen Markham was basically a considerate man. In spite of his differences with his family, he was concerned for their welfare. He winterized their living quarters and even constructed a chimney higher than the roof so they could at last do their cooking inside.

Even in cold, miserable conditions, homeless and with but the most meager of provisions, the Saints found ways to cheer one another and keep their spirits light.

Eliza loved visiting her friends. In late December, 1846, she left the Markham cabin for a five-day visit with Loisa Decker, Patty Sessions and Zina D. H. Young. During that time, "the girls," as they called themselves, revived a practice they had put aside for many months. Joyful to be together, they felt a bond of love and unity. Into that pure atmosphere, the Lord poured out his spirit, and the women began speaking and blessing one another in tongues.

Of a New Year's party given by Patty Sessions, Eliza wrote, "Last eve we had a very interesting time to close my five day visit with the girls, for whom my love seem'd to increase with every day's acquaintance. To describe the scene alluded to would be beyond my pow'r—suffice it to say, the spirit of the Lord was pour'd out and we receiv'd a blessing thro' our belov'd Mother Chase, and sis. Clarissa by the gift of tongues."

From a comparison of individual diaries, it appears that Patty Sessions was probably the original leader in organizing such spiritual meetings among the women. Patty was the most prominent midwife among the Mormons in the mid-nineteenth century. Not only did she assist in childbirth, but she also doctored other illnesses, using herbs and poultices available to her on the plains.

In both circumstances, illness or childbirth, Patty supplemented her nursing skills with what she considered a higher form of medicine: spiritual healing. In present-day Mormon custom only the male members (priesthood holders) normally are permitted to lay hands upon the sick and administer to them, anointing with consecrated oil as they do so; but in Eliza's day, women also performed such ordinances, and Patty Sessions more than others.

That New Year's party on the first day of 1847 seemed to be a catalyst, infusing Eliza with the heady realization of her spiritual powers. From that day to the end of her life she would refer often in her journals to similar spiritual experiences. It is interesting to note that as she gained experience and her confidence grew, she steadily progressed from being an excited participant to being a leader of the group, until on Sunday, May 2, she recorded, "This eve supp'd at sis. Noon's with sis. Kim [Kimball], Whit [Whitney], Ses [Sessions], Lyon, Sara A., Helen, etc. Had as glorious a time as I ever had on earth at Sis K [Kimball]'s—myself chosen to preside—the pow'rs of the world to come were truly in our midst."

During an otherwise tedious and colorless season, Eliza and her friends filled their days and evenings with "blessing parties." The meetings steadily increased in frequency until soon all the inhabitants of Winter Quarters were aware of the parties.

For two reasons, however, some of the brethren of the camp began to be uneasy about the spiritual gatherings. No doubt they recalled the restriction the prophet Joseph Smith had placed on the members, cautioning them about their preoccupation with speaking in tongues and limiting their use of the gift to one hour a month in the Kirtland Temple. In addition to that reservation, it became apparent that there were hurt feelings on the part of those not included in Eliza's select group. To be sure, the "blessing parties" were not limited to women. Often Brigham Young, Heber C. Kimball and husbands of Eliza's special friends were present as well. But, true to the trend of human nature, Eliza was very much a part of a special circle of dynamic individuals, wives of leaders, and leaders in their own right. Without intending to exclude anyone, these outstanding people naturally gravitated to each other, forming, in the minds of the outsiders, a clique.

In a later diary entry Patty Sessions recorded, "Father Abot called again. Told me Sister Leonard said that there was as good sisters as I was and she could have a meeting without me or Sister Snow. He also said that Mary Pratt had been misrepreting [misrepresenting] some of our words that we said at sister Cotchners [Kartchner's] carying [sic] the idea that we thought we stopped [sic] very low to visit her. This we know was false."

The disapproval of the brethren, Patriarch John Smith in particular, worried the sisters. Not wanting to be in disfavor, they invited brother Smith to join them frequently, but the invitation only caused him to feel that they were trying to take advantage of him. Even as much as a year later, his misgivings persisted. Finally, to smooth over bad feelings, Patty and Eliza visited the aged patriarch, taking some fried cakes and a cap Eliza had made. They must have been successful in their peace offering, for Patty wrote, "He blessed me and said many good things to me and we left with good feelings."

Far more than mere disapproval would have been necessary to halt the meetings of those spiritually motivated women. The frequency of their gatherings increased until they were being held daily, at times two and more times a day just prior to Eliza's departure from Winter Quarters on June 12, 1847. Carol Lynn Pearson, a Mormon author, has noted in her book, *Daughters of Light*, the experiences of the last twelve days before Eliza left with the Pierce family on the last leg of her journey to Utah. To quote Eliza:

"Tuesday, June 1. This is truly a glorious time with the mothers and daughters of Zion, altho' thrust out from the land of our forefathers and from endearments of civiliz'd life. This forenoon I made a cap for sis. Peirce; in the afternoon I visited at sis. Miller's, in com [company] of Priscinda, sis. Chase, Cristene [sic], etc. After supper sis. Whitney, Kimball [and] Sessions came in and we had a spiritual feast in very deed. Spent the eve at br. Leonard's with Priscinda, Zina and Sarah—great instruction was brought forth....

"Wednesday, June 2. Spent the after [afternoon] with Lucy in com [company] of Zina, Loisa and Emily. E [Emily] and myself spoke in the gift of tongues. In the eve, met at Harriet's; had a good time—Sis. Young join'd me in a song of Zion.

"Thursday, June 3. Sis. Sess [Sessions], Kim [Kimball], Whit [Whitney] and myself spent the eve at Sarah Ann's—had a pow'rful time—deep things were brought forth which were not to be spoken.

"Friday, June 4. We had a very pleasant visit at br. Leonard's. Present: br. Joseph [Young] and wife, br. Sess [Sessions] and wife, sis. Whitney, Kimball, etc. I blest sis. Young.

"Saturday, June 5. Fath [Father] Sess [Sessions] leaves for the wilderness. I attended meeting at sis. Leavitt's.

"Sunday, June 6. Had a glorious time at sis. Young's. Present: sis Whit [Whitney], Kim [Kimball], Chase, etc. I had forgotten to mention a time of blessing at sis. K [Kimball]'s the day after we met at Sarah's. Sis Sess [Sessions] and myself blest Helen. I spoke and she interpreted. I then blest the girls in a song, singing to each in rotation.

"In the eve. that we met at Harriet's, sis. Young told me she thought wisdom for me to go to the west, inasmuch as I could go so comfortable with br. Peirce. Sis. P [Peirce] had mention'd her wish for me to go with them, in his absence, but had not yet decided whether his means would permit.

"Monday, June 7. Met at sis. Woodruff's in the afternoon—at br. Leonard's in the even. Moth [Mother] Butler receiv'd the gift of tongues. Sis. Scovil present.

"Tuesday, June 8. Met at Lyman Whitney's, stay'd in the eve., had a heavy shower of rain—went home with Loisa and Z [Zina] in the mud rejoicing.

"Wednesday, June 9. Visited with Zina, Martha, L [Loisa], E [Emily], Lucy, Eliza and Sarah. After supper we had a glorious time. Sis. Peirce came in—sis. Thompson, M. Jones and Francis. Before we retir'd to rest, Margaret, Martha, Loisa, Susan and Lucy reciv'd the gift of tongues.

"Thursday, June 10. In the mor [morning] met sis. Chase at Clarissa's—blest her little daughter which was born last Tu [Tuesday]. Told Harriet she would get the gift of interpretation in the eve. In the aft [afternoon] call'd at sis. Woodru [Woodruff's] and Priscinda's and went to br. Moore's where sis. Whit [Whitney]'s girls met, sent for Zina, Harriet came with her. Sis. Richards, Rhonda, Emeline, Anna, and one of sis. M [Markham]'s daughters spoke in the gift for the first time. Took supper with S [Sarah] Ann K [Kimball]. While there Lucy W [Walker] came in— she receiv'd the gift. We then went into sis. K [Kimball]'s—Helen, Sarah Ann, Genet, Harriet S., sis. K [Kimball] spoke for the first time in the gift of tongues—H. Cook interpreted.

"Friday, June 11. Sent for Harriet—we commenc'd improving in the gifts—Helen got the interpretation, also sis. W. Mary Ellen spoke in a new tongue, sis. Pack also—we had a time not to be forgotten. In the aft. met at Clarissa's—sis. Snow [Lorenzo's wife] receiv'd the gift before we left Loisa's. We had a glorious time—sis. Levitt and M [Margaret] Peirce spoke in the gift and I could truly say that my heart was fill'd to overflowing with gratitude to my Father in heaven.

"Saturday, June 12. Bade farewell to many who seemed dearer to me than life and, seated in the carriage with sis. P [Peirce], M [Margaret] and E [Eli] I took my departure from Winter Quarters."

And so it went, day after day, all the way to the valley of the mountains. Eliza was in and out of tents and wagons, blessing, singing songs of Zion wherever she went, always in the pure Adamic language, or "Eve's tongue" as she called it. Historians have speculated about Eliza and her friends, those remarkable women, and their unusual experiences with the gift of tongues. Were they *so* much more spiritual than even the strong Latter-day Saint leaders of today? Are modern-day Mormons more inhibited, consequently shutting themselves off from such deeply moving opportunities? Perhaps the answer is simply that Eliza and her sisters desperately *needed* the strength and refreshment those spiritual feasts provided. Their hardships were so overwhelming that without such uplifting moments, they may well have fainted by the way.

But faint Eliza did not. In fact, she was far from weak during the final phase of that marathon westward trek. Her strength and enthusiasm grew as her company neared its destination. She wrote of eating antelope and buffalo meat, proclaiming them a treat. Her excitement ran high each time a message was found beside the trail, inscribed on a buffalo skull or a plank of wood by a preceding company. With courage she met new experiences, such as the constant danger from Indians. Again and again Eliza wrote of the breathtaking beauty of the scenes surrounding her, the high Scott's Bluffs, the celebrated Black Hills, Independence Rock and Devil's Gate, where thousands of travelers carved their names during the covered wagon era. She forded the Platte River so many times as it twisted and doubled back over the trail that she wrote, "It was like meeting an old friend."

On Friday, September 10, Brigham Young, on his way back to Winter Quarters to pick up the remainder of his family, stopped by Eliza's carriage and blessed her. Concerned about where she would live and who would be responsible for her keep, Eliza recorded their light conversation about the matter: "I asked who was to be my counselor for the year to come—He said E [Eliza] R. S [Snow]. I said, 'She is not capable.' He said, 'I have appointed her president. . . .'" Although Brigham made arrangements for her to live with Clara Decker Young, one of his wives and Eliza's good friend, his jovial remark revealed his awareness of Eliza's emerging qualities. Always gifted and intelligent, the rigors of her journey had forged new strengths in her character. The Eliza R. Snow who soon settled into the fort in what is now Salt Lake City, Utah, was a builder, a leader, an organizer, well prepared for the new phase of her life which was about to unfold before her.

Chapter Eleven

President Young seemed to extend himself beyond what was expected when it came to looking after Eliza. That first winter in the valley, he placed her as he had promised, with Clara Decker, who had arrived in the vanguard group known as the pioneers' mid-summer company. President Young had constructed a fort with log rooms or houses 18 feet square. A flat roof made of mud and grass kept out the sun and cold as Eliza settled in with Clara for the winter of 1847.

Eliza seemed in hearty spirits as she described that season. "Our first winter in the mountains was delightful; the ground froze but little; our coldest weather was three or four days in November, after which the men plowed and sowed, built houses, etc. The weather seemed to have been particularly ordered to meet our very peculiar circumstances."

The task of creating a settlement out of raw materials on dry soil was never easy, as Eliza readily admitted: "Every labor, such as cultivating the ground, procuring fuel and timber from the canyons, etc., was a matter of experiment. Most of us were houseless; and what the result would have been, had that winter been like the succeeding ones, may well be conjectured."

Though the winter was mild, conditions were anything but ideal. Living in the tiny log house on the endless flat of the valley was little better than staying in a tent. In fact, during an early spring downpour, Eliza and Clara must have wished they had remained in a dry tent. According to Eliza, their "hut, like most of those built the first year, was roofed with willows and earth, the roof having but little pitch, the first comers having adopted the idea that the valley was subject to little if any rain, and our roofs were nearly flat. We suffered no inconvenience from this fact until about the middle of March, when a long storm of snow, sleet and rain occurred, and for several days the sun did not make its appearance. The roof of our dwelling was covered deeper with earth than the adjoining ones, consequently it did not leak so soon, and some of my neighbors huddled in for shelter; but one evening, when several were socially sitting around, the water commenced dripping in one place, and then in another; they dodged it for awhile, but it increased so rapidly that they finally concluded they might as well go to their own wet houses."

Eliza seemed philosophical and resigned to her dripping wet circumstances as she bid the neighbors goodnight. Then, with the dignity of a well-bred lady, she unfolded her large umbrella and seated herself squarely in bed, placing the umbrella over her head to shield her upper body. Thus covering herself, she settled in for the night with apparently no thought of discouragement. By morning, she said, "The earth overhead was thoroughly saturated, and after it commenced to drip the storm was much worse indoors than out."

Some felt nothing but hardship and added stress to the settlement by complaining about conditions, but Eliza refused to find fault, either with nature or the leaders. Long before, she had accepted the fact that conditions would be uncomfortable. But she knew that what the Mormons were experiencing was what the Lord intended for their best good, and that was sufficient for Eliza.

Food was scarce and precious to the struggling Saints. The gift of a small item of food such as a jar of beans or a tin of tea was cause to rejoice.

Soon after her company had arrived, Eliza knitted a night cap for John Young's wife. She noted the fact in her journal, adding,

"...for which she paid me in soap, one pound and 15 ounces—so much I call my own—I now begin once more to be a woman of property."

Before the vanguard group had pulled out of Winter Quarters, a general inspection of wagons had been ordered to ascertain that every family heading west possessed a sufficient amount of goods. They were expected to have three-quarters of a pound of meal per day for each adult; for the children, half a pound. That would have been fine, had the Saints' numbers remained the same. But by late winter, the disbanded Mormon Battalion, its members destitute because they had received no mustering-out pay, and with no reserves of food, joined the new Mormon community. Of course the men were given portions from the settlers. Eliza said they "joined us before spring, and we cheerfully divided our rations of flour with them, which put us on still shorter allowance."

Still Eliza did not complain, perhaps because she too had been dependent on the generosity of others so often during the past years.

Though the Saints' first years in their mountain retreat were years of hardship and struggle, at last a real city began to take shape.

Eliza had little to do with the actual physical labor of constructing housing, roads, public and commercial buildings and a host of improvements that were undertaken the first decade in the valley. She, like most women of her temperament and training, tended to household tasks and the care of those who did the back-breaking work to transform the valley into a productive, civilized city of commerce.

Surely Eliza gloried in every new structure that arose from the desert floor. She had first seen the valley just short weeks after the pioneers had planted the few tiny trees which they had carefully transported across the plains. The fine farms that gradually appeared on every side looked much different than the two or three planted fields she had first observed.

It is interesting to note what Eliza's husband, Brigham Young, had amassed on Block 89 in Salt Lake City by the spring of 1855. In his "Deed" of holdings, Brigham Young wrote concerning his primary residence in the heart of the city, "Block

89 in Great Salt Lake City Survey, with all the buildings and improvements thereon, consisting of 'White House,' Barn, one Row of Log Houses [one log house being a residence for Eliza], one small adobe house, one milk house, one smoke house, one corn house, and garden, entire value, $25,000. Lots 1 and 2 south quarter of lots 7 and 8 in block 88, one large house [main residence that stands today on South Temple], garden, and a small Doby Shoe Shop and log house, value $60,000."

Eliza undoubtedly never felt that any of her husband's possessions were hers, or that she would ever be entitled to claim any part of his far-flung holdings.

But Brigham Young, a firm believer in communal living, handed over his possessions to the church in a special Deed of Consecration. He felt strongly that members ought to enter voluntarily in the economic order of communal holdings called the Law of Consecration. The voluntary act of giving over to the church all of one's earthly goods—in his case listed in detail to be such items as "one gold watch at $50"—never swept the church and thus failed to ignite the truest order of giving, though Brigham Young himself set the pattern.

In the way of material possessions, what Brigham Young did for Eliza, as well as for his several other wives, was to leave them a comfortable home and security for life. Because material goods and land had never been a serious concern for Eliza, she seldom mentioned what she possessed or lacked of this world's goods. But it surely must have been comforting to watch her husband's expanding estate and know she would always share in the growing prosperity.

Whereas Joseph, her first husband, had been a visionary man filled with a drive to expand the mind and soul of humankind, Brigham, her second mate, stood foremost in America as an empire builder. Each was vital to his era. The Lord had worked through the sensitive, charismatic prophet, Joseph Smith, to reestablish His church and to touch the hearts of truth-seeking men, drawing them into the body of the members. But Brigham Young's skills were also essential. He organized a system of living that made practical sense to the growing number of immigrants who flocked into the Mormon lands to put down deep roots.

Brigham had grand visions of creating a vast Mormon empire. Little time passed before he called men to take their families and colonize other areas. One group was sent to southern Idaho, another to Arizona. Certain brethren were sent to the warmer climate of southern Utah to experiment in cotton production. Brigham's desire was that the church be totally self-sufficient—dependent on potentially hostile outsiders for as little as possible. So Mormons were encouraged to produce a variety of goods, even cotton, wool and silk for their clothing.

It was during that colonizing period that President Young sent Lorenzo Snow, by then one of the 12 apostles, to Box Elder County, some 60 miles north of Salt Lake City, to be in charge of 50 families there. Several families had been sent prior to Lorenzo's call. But, according to Eliza, "[the settlement] had lost every vestige of enterprise and was minus every aim in the direction of advancement. To diffuse active energies and a spirit of progress into this stereotyped condition of people, was not unlike raising the dead."

Lorenzo, usually a cheerful, positive leader, was all but discouraged by the task before him. He observed, "Even the log meeting house, with its ground floor and earth roof, was more of a receptacle for bedbugs than for the assemblage of Saints."

Lorenzo's family had steadily increased from the time he was in charge of the Saints at Mt. Pisgah when three of his wives bore children in rapid succession. Initially, when called to colonize the Box Elder area, Lorenzo took only part of his family. But soon he had erected a house 30 feet by 40, one and one-half stories high. Into this home he settled all his wives and children.

Though seemingly an impossible task, Lorenzo Snow soon transformed the apathetic farmers of his little community into energetic, industrious Saints. He named their newly thriving settlement Brigham City, in honor of the man he admired more than any.

Brigham's taste for grandeur was not limited to colonizing. It extended to his personal lifestyle as well.

By 1855, plans had been drawn up for a proper home for the president of the church and part of his families. During the winter of 1854, Brigham Young had participated in planning sessions to help design his residence. He envisioned a large plantation-like structure for his home and office.

The long, narrow building called the Lion House was of New England design with a steep-pitched roof and 20 dormer windows placed along the east and west sides of the roof. Its foundation of red sandstone and sturdy walls of sun-baked six-inch adobe bricks, formed and baked on the Young property, became the living quarters for Brigham Young's wives and children.

Because no native hardwoods grew in the mountains, hired craftsmen applied a technique called "graining" to the indigenous pine. Many of the converts from Europe were skilled in this craft. The result was very close in appearance to the hardwoods of New England. Those who finished the tabernacle applied the same method a few years later.

Glass for the windows of the Lion House came all the way from the East Coast. When compared with modern glass, the panes were imperfect, creating a distorted view. The women of the family wove rugs made of dyed wool for the halls and sitting room. But the family sent away for a store-bought carpet to adorn the parlor.

The Lion House must have seemed more like a fine hotel than a home for one man's family. How large and elegant it was, with a wide central hall running the length of the house on each of the three floors.

The basement floor housed the mechanics of everyday tasks and living. There, a pantry and a large kitchen with massive stoves, stone hearths and ovens were capable of supplying food on a daily basis for up to 75 people. To one side in the cavern-like cellar, surrounded by cool stones, stood pans of milk and cream, freshly churned butter and homemade cheeses. To the rear of the kitchen was a laundry room, complete with a stove and large vats for boiling and rinsing the family clothing. Brigham employed at least one man at all times to carry the heavy buckets of water from the backyard well and to pound the clothes. A school was located in a northeast basement room, and it was usually taught by one of the wives. Surely Eliza took her turn. A large dining room, whose long tables regularly seated the family of 50-plus for daily meals, stretched out at the opposite end of the hall.

On the main floor, a long parlor or prayer room was elegantly furnished with Nottingham lace at the deep paneled windows. Twenty bedroom apartments were situated across from the parlor and upstairs on the third floor. By the 1860s Brigham had built a gymnasium the length of the west wall.

During Eliza's lifetime at the Lion House, a glassed-in

vestibule kept out the cold air of winter. It became customary for each person who went out in the evening to place his or her individual coal-oil lamp on the window sill or on a table placed in the vestibule for that purpose. As many as 25 lamps would line the room on a festive evening. Upon arriving home, each person would pick up his or her own lighted lamp and slip upstairs to bed. The person who got back to find only one lamp left, would know that all the others were home. His or her duty was then to lock the door and extinguish the hall lamp.

A stream of handsome young men passed through the vestibule to the parlor, to visit the young ladies of the house. At one time, in the 1860s, Brigham Young's 10 oldest daughters, very close in age, were all being courted by young men at the same time. The girls were fondly called "the big ten." They were given the privilege of entertaining their beaux each Sunday evening in the parlor. Brigham Young approved of the weekly gatherings, so long as high standards were maintained.

Feeling that the lamp in the center of the room was much too bright, one Sunday evening the boys turned the lamp down, dimming it as much as possible. Not quite satisfied yet, they stacked books to make a barricade around the lamp. All went well for a while, until the door opened and the girls' father, Brigham Young, stood in the doorway with a lighted candle in his hand. He took one look around the room and walked to the table, where he removed the books one by one and turned up the lamp. Then, facing the chagrined young people, he declared, "The girls will go to their rooms and I will say good night to the young men."

Eliza was certainly in agreement with President Young's firmness in maintaining high morals. In fact, she was in complete harmony with the formality of the Young household. She knew the life pattern of President Young and seemed to find contentment in its routine. Though the Lion House was constantly bustling with activity—a situation to be expected with so many children—the family's routines reflected an orderliness that stemmed from strong leadership. The whole family gathered early each evening for the dinner meal in the basement-level dining room. Sometimes more than 50 persons dined together. All the wives and their several children would be present, with the frequent addition of Lorenzo and Joseph Young, brothers of President Young, and usually an invited guest or two. The food would be spread on at least five tables and certain members of the family, by assignment, would help serve the meal which had been prepared by several of the wives.

Always, Eliza sat to the right of President Young at the head dinner table. It was she who set the style of grace and manners. Meals were eaten leisurely with lively conversation. Listening to the day's events tumble from the lips of President Young, who was not only president of the church, but the territorial governor as well, must have been intriguing to everyone present.

Eliza was able to inform the president of her ventures and offer her views on current issues. Even in that casual way, she had impact on his opinions.

Following the early dinner, there were set chores to perform for the wives and studies for the children. In about an hour, President Young would return from his office, where he often worked following the meal, to the parlor of the Lion House. At seven o'clock in the evening, Eliza would hear from her third-floor apartment the ringing of the large prayer bell. She was never without some small task to perform, stitching, writing or talking with one of the young ladies of the house.

Sometimes, if the prayer bell failed to arouse certain members of the household, President Young would quietly step to several of the third-floor apartments and signal the advent of prayer time in person.

In the prayer parlor, with its mirrors and ornate windows skirted by the Nottingham lace, President Young would seat himself in the center of the room on one of the fine straight-backed padded chairs. He was often flanked by his brothers, Joseph and Lorenzo, who made it a custom to be in the parlor at prayer time, though they lived up the street from the Lion House. In mere moments, the rustle of skirts and the patter of feet could be heard as family members would gather from all corners of the house for prayer.

Eliza would be one of the first to come swishing into the room. Clarissa Young Spencer, one of Brigham's daughters, remembered "Aunt Eliza" with a special fondness. "She was slight and fragile," Clarissa said, "...and always immaculate in dress. I see her now in her full-skirted, lace trimmed silk dresses, with her dainty lace caps and a gold chain around her neck, looking for all the world like a piece of Dresden china." Eliza would quietly seat herself to the right of the president, next to his brother. If the brothers were absent, then she sat at President Young's immediate right as the entire family prepared to pray, each wife and her children in their accustomed places.

According to Clarissa, her father would usually choose a topic and deliver a mini-discourse on the subject, usually an issue of the day. Following the brief discussion, "We would all join in singing some familiar songs, either old-time ballads or songs of religious nature. Finally we would all kneel down while Father offered the evening prayers." Clarissa remembered for the rest of her life one distinct phrase in her father's prayer, "Bless the church and thy people, the sick and the afflicted and comfort the hearts that mourn."

After prayer, if no social events such as meetings, concerts or plays were scheduled, most would arise and scatter to their individual apartments or go off to visit friends. The wives would often gather in their sitting rooms to talk and sew together after putting their younger children to bed.

For Eliza, evening was often a time of personal organization. She sat at her desk by the window and planned meetings, outlined speeches, wrote letters and *always* penned her much-loved verses. From all available diaries, it would appear that all of Brigham's wives held Eliza in great esteem. Especially did the young ladies admire her, in spite of her rather strict ways.

Said Clarissa of her Aunt Eliza R. Snow, "She held a most honored place in our household and indeed in the whole community, for it is doubtful if the church has ever produced any woman who was her superior."

Eliza—A Complex Woman

Chapter Twelve

As the Saints began to make headway in their herculean task of building Salt Lake City and the surrounding settlements, their just reward was the luxury of a little spare time. To be sure, there was always much work to be done, but orderliness and schedule replaced the feverish 'round-the-clock pace of the early years.

Few records indicate Eliza's activities during her first seven years in the valley. Knowing Eliza, we can imagine her knitting caps, braiding straw for hats and calling on her friends. As at Winter Quarters, "blessing parties" were prevalent, including men as well as women. In many diary accounts, Eliza's name is listed as a participant, continuing to bless and sing in tongues.

On July 7, 1852, under instructions from Brigham Young, Heber C. Kimball resumed the administration of endowment ordinances, which had begun in the temple in Nauvoo some six years earlier. Having, as yet, no temple, the Saints used the "Old Council House" for the sacred rites until a proper endowment house could be constructed. As high priestess of the church, Eliza presided over and instructed the women who administered the ordinances to their sisters. This responsibility alone must have occupied a great deal of her time.

Eliza also continued to practice her literary skills. Scarcely a program or a ceremony was held in the valley that did not include a poem or a song written by her favored pen.

The first major celebration held in the territory of Utah was on July 24, 1849, the second anniversary of the pioneers' entrance to the Salt Lake Valley. Eliza's brother, Lorenzo, had been placed in charge of the entire event. Eliza was generous with her praise of Lorenzo's efforts. "They had 'the right man in the right place,' for in this instance as in everything he undertook, Lorenzo verified the adage, 'What is worth doing, is worth doing well.' And, to make a success of whatever he undertook, he neither spared labor nor application."

Eliza described the commemorative ceremony in minute detail in her biography of her brother: "The inhabitants were awakened by the firing of cannon, accompanied by music. The brass band, playing martial airs, paraded the principal streets of the city, in a gaily decorated omnibus, with prancing steeds, and with banners flying . . ."

At eight o'clock in the morning, following the raising of a large national flag, the Saints gathered in the open-air Bowery for the program. The Bowery, attached to the north side of the tabernacle, had been constructed to serve as a meeting place when the number of inhabitants outgrew the tabernacle's capacity. Measuring 100 feet long and 60 feet wide, the structure featured 104 posts supporting a ramada-type roof which was covered with brush to provide a shade. For the 1849 anniversary occasion, 100-foot awnings were extended from each side to accommodate the vast multitude for the program and dinner.

In a magnificent display of pomp and ceremony, Lorenzo Snow, Jedediah M. Grant and Franklin D. Richards led an escort party, marching between lines of admiring supporters to the residence of Brigham Young. It is certain that Eliza added her touch to the imposing cortege. She listed the escort by number: "(1) Horace S. Eldredge, Marshal, on horseback, in military uniform; (2) brass band; (3) twelve Bishops, bearing the banners of their wards; (4) twenty-four young men dressed in white pants, black coats, white scarfs [sic] on the right shoulder, and coronets on their heads, each carrying in his right hand a copy of the Declaration of Independence, and the Constitution of the

United States, and each wearing a sheathed sword by his side—
one of them carrying a beautiful banner, on which was inscribed,
'The Lion of the Lord;' (5) twenty-four young ladies dressed in
white, with blue scarfs [sic] on the right shoulder, and with
wreaths of white roses on their heads, each carrying a Bible and a
Book of Mormon, and one carrying a neat banner, inscribed with
'Hail to our Captain;' (6) P. P. Pratt, John Taylor, Charles C. Rich,
Daniel Spencer, David Fullmer, Willard Snow, Erastus Snow; (7)
twenty-four silver Greys [older men] led by Isaac Morley,
Patriarch—each carrying the 'Stars and Stripes,' bearing the
inscription, 'LIBERTY OR DEATH.'"

At the president's home, the grand escort party led Brigham
Young and Heber C. Kimball, followed by the 12 apostles, back to
the Bowery, all the while accompanied by the ringing of the
"Nauvoo bell," the discharging of cannon and muskets, and "the
soul-stirring strains of the brass band." As they marched, the 24
young men and 24 young women sang "The Mountain
Standard," a piece written by Apostle Parley P. Pratt.

Brigham Young and his party were received by the crowd
with unison shouts of "Hosanna to God and the Lamb" and "Hail
to the Governor of Deseret." A long and patriotic program
followed, including a song written by Eliza R. Snow which was
sung by the 24 lovely young ladies dressed in white.

Song of Liberty

Long, long ago, when Earth and Time
Were in the morn of life,
All joyous in their lovely prime,
With fragrant beauty rife.
All nature then in order crowned
With perfect harmony;
Luxuriant products clothed the ground,
O, there was Liberty.

No vail [sic] obscured the worlds on high
From those that dwelt on earth;
But in the pathway of the sky,
They journeyed back and forth.
Then God and angels talked with men,
And woman, too, was free,
For both were pure and sinless then,
In perfect liberty.

The curse pursued transgression's track,
And man from God was driven,
Until the Priesthood brought him back,
To do the will of heaven.
We'll shout Hosanna to the Lord
For what is yet to be,
When earth and man will be restored
To God and liberty.

We see the lighthouse brightly blaze
Far o'er the boisterous wave;
With cheering prospects thus we gaze
On hopes beyond the grave;
For woman, if submissive here
To God's divine decree,
Restored will fill a noble sphere
In glorious liberty.

The Lord has set his gracious hand,
And by His mighty power,
He led his people to this land—
Preparing for the hour;
For Earth and Time are growing old,
And soon Eternity
Will to the Saints of God unfold
CELESTIAL LIBERTY.

At the conclusion of the final speech and one more of Eliza's songs, "Ode to Liberty," the entire throng enjoyed a feast, the members of each ward being led to their assigned tables by their bishop. Eliza wrote: "Thousands of Saints dined sumptuously on the products of the valley, judiciously and delicately prepared, and rendered delicious in connection with what foreign luxuries as were obtained in exchange for staple articles, as flour, butter, potatoes, etc., from travelers to California."

The festivities were so exciting, so well received by all, that the 24th of July became an official Mormon holiday. Saints today celebrate the occasion all over the world with parades and picnics and pioneer displays.

As in Nauvoo, when a measure of prosperity had replaced soul-shrinking destitution, the rejoicing Latter-day Saints soon became hungry for a social life, for culture and for intellectual discussions. One of the first buildings erected in the city was the Social Hall, whose purposes were just what its name implied. The

Mormons held balls, feasts, plays and birthday celebrations in the Social Hall. Because few meeting places existed, the Saints also put it to use for more serious gatherings, such as sessions of the territorial legislature or priesthood council meetings. Eliza attended many gala affairs in the Social Hall. But by comparison to cities east of the Mississippi, Salt Lake City offered little to stimulate the mind.

Historian Maureen Ursenbach Beecher poses a question: "What was there for any woman of intellect in Utah in the 1850s? There was a kind of intellectual sisterhood for one thing," she decided. "Women of similar interests, then as now, were naturally drawn together: new mothers clustered to talk about their babies; musical women congregated to sing and play; seamstresses gathered around the quilting frames; and women who lived the life of the mind sought each other."

Among these intellectual sisters, Hannah Tapfield King, Martha Spence Heywood and Eliza Roxcy Snow comprised the nucleus of the group. But there were men also who desired mental stimulation. In 1854, Eliza's own brother, Lorenzo, led out in the formation of a new society which he called the Polysophical Association.

"It was," wrote Eliza, "in the form of a series of evening entertainments, consisting of a most remarkable combination of physical, moral, mental and spiritual exercises, all blended in one harmonious whole."

The association met every two weeks to enjoy a varied-interest program. Lorenzo and those he consulted were very careful to alternate musical numbers with the spoken word, humorous with more serious endeavors. All participants were invited in advance to perform, to allow them sufficient time for preparation. Lorenzo appointed a master of ceremonies for each program, providing a table and chair for that designated person in the center of the hall. As the evening progressed, the master of ceremonies would dispatch notes, carried by a small boy, to the performers, informing each of the precise time to come forward and present his offering.

Eliza observed, "During the exercises the attention of all was so firmly riveted that apparently no one in the audience felt any inclination to leave a seat, speak or whisper, but an all absorbing heed was directed to each contributed portion of the magnificent moral, intellectual and spiritual picnic."

In a very short time, the fame of the association spread throughout the city. Soon Lorenzo had accepted as many members as he could accommodate in his large home. Still, eager friends begged to be admitted to the group. At length the programs were held in the Seventies Hall or sometimes in the Social Hall.

What seemed to be the perfect answer to the needs of an intellectually starved people was, unfortunately, soon to be extinguished. Even though President Brigham Young had participated at times in the society's programs, thus lending his approval to the group, a reformation movement led by Jedediah M. Grant, one of Brigham Young's counselors, surfaced to stamp out all evil. Sad to say, Brother Grant thought he saw the roots of evil in the Polysophical Association.

In her journal, Hannah Tapfield King observed bitterly, "Brother Grant has done some strong preaching lately, and declared the Polysophical Society was 'a stink in his nostrils.' Brother Kimball called out, 'and in mine!' Said there was an adulterous spirit in it!! Well, there may be, for he says there is, and probably he understands it. To me it all seemed good and nice, with of course a little vanity and folly, and that one sees in the tabernacle and everywhere."

The charter chapter of the association in Salt Lake City was replaced less than two years after its inception by a church-controlled organization named the Deseret Theological Class, personally directed by Brigham Young. Because the class lacked the vitality, the excitement and yes, the support of the former Polysophical officials, it lasted only a year and then faded into oblivion.

One can only imagine the feelings of Eliza concerning the accusation that an adulterous spirit existed in a fellowship in which she was so closely associated. Conjecture leads us to suppose that the jealousy of non-participants may have been the underlying problem. Throughout her life, Eliza moved within the center of the elite, whether shivering in a covered wagon or safely enthroned in the princely Lion House. Without doubt there were those who felt unaccepted, unable to compete intellectually with the high society which comprised the Polysophical Association. Sufficient numbers of complaints and rumors may have caused the intense suspicion felt by Jedediah Grant and Heber Kimball.

The effort toward culture and improvement of minds was hardly squelched. Other branches of the Polysophical Association in outlying communities in the territory continued to flourish. Even in Salt Lake City proper, other musical and literary groups were gradually organized.

Another type of intellectual expression took the form of theatrical productions. Again, Eliza's brother was heavily involved. When Lorenzo removed his family to Brigham City and found such dejection among the inhabitants, he built a theatre at Eliza's suggestion and encouraged the whole settlement to participate in its plays. The results were astonishing. The plays stimulated energy and interest which carried over to other areas of living. Soon the community was thriving and even the formerly apathetic farmers were prospering.

Eliza *always* followed the counsel of the priesthood-bearing leaders. Whatever her feelings at the demise of the Polysophical Association, we are safe to believe that no critical words escaped her lips. Instead, she conformed her own opinions to coincide with those voiced by the hierarchy of the church. Speaking to a gathering of young women in 1875, she said: "Literary Associations are good in their way, but it is spiritual culture, spiritual food the young want . . . Does the education of the world prepare you . . . to associate in the holy order of the house of God? No, it only fits you to be ornaments in Babylon."

Another time, Eliza wrote: "What is true greatness? In human character, usefulness constitutes greatness . . . In the estimation of holy intelligences, the most useful character or person is the greatest . . . The glory of God is his works." Surely her reading audience was puzzled by her alteration of the Doctrine and Covenants scripture which read, "The glory of God is intelligence."

Despite her expressions to the contrary, Eliza would continue all her life to improve her mind, express her talents and encourage others to follow her lead.

Even in a society where, according to one historian, "novel reading was discouraged; antiprofessionalism, especially against lawyers and doctors was a prevailing attitude," Eliza and her kindred spirits would never be completely silenced. For the remainder of her life, Eliza would be a leader, culturally, socially and indeed, intellectually too.

Chapter Thirteen

By the 1860s, great change had come to the valley of the mountains. Salt Lake City was thriving, the church was firmly established and growing. Eliza too had grown and changed. There was an air of confidence and determination about her that surely she had been born with, but it had gradually emerged and was now apparent to all. No longer did Eliza seat herself in a corner and for long periods compose poetry. She was now on the move. There was much to be done to build the kingdom of God.

Eliza was ever willing to pull her share; this Brigham knew, and he began to make use of her unique abilities. Time after time, he called on her to take positions of responsibility until she became, under his direction, the most powerful woman in the church. Indeed Eliza was so well loved by her sisters and so endowed with the ability to lead and to sway others that she eventually became Brigham Young's liaison with all the female portion of the church. Most historians agree that Eliza probably had as much if not more influence on the church than did either of Brigham Young's counselors, considering that, as a wife, Eliza had ready access to Brigham's ear and that the great leader often heeded the quiet suggestions she offered.

Perhaps the prime responsibility Brigham gave to Eliza was in 1866 to organize once more a Relief Society among the sisters. When the Saints had fled Nauvoo, the organization had been dissolved. Though in each company of pioneers during the exodus west, women had continued to serve one another in a charitable manner, there was no official direction. When the Saints had first arrived in the valley, they had been appalled by the living conditions they found among the Indians whose camps were nearby. Again, on a voluntary basis, many of the Mormon women took pity on the Indians, and gathered in sewing circles to clothe them. Calling their groups "Indian Relief Societies," they met often, teaching the Indian women homemaking skills and basic principles of cleanliness. However, the Indians, notably the Arrapeen and Sanpitch tribes, were nomadic. They had soon moved on and the Indian Relief Societies were discontinued.

It was obvious that the women hungered for a group of their own, a means to satisfy their natural desires to be social as well as to give service. By 1858, a number of ladies' groups had been organized through central and northern Utah where settlements had been established.

Knowing of the good the women had accomplished in Nauvoo, and also aware of the need for a uniform organization throughout the spreading church, Brigham reactivated the Relief Society. He not only chose Eliza to head it up, but instructed all bishops in the growing wards to organize branches of the women's group as Eliza would direct.

After Eliza had been sustained by the unanimous vote of the sisters attending the Ladies' Quarterly Conference held in the Assembly Hall, President John Taylor ordained her to the office of Relief Society President over all the women in the church and blessed her in these words:

"Eliza Roxcy Snow Smith, I lay my hands upon thy head in the name of Jesus, and by the authority of the Holy Priesthood I set thee apart to preside over the Relief Societies of the Church of Jesus Christ of Latter-day Saints, and I confer upon thee this power and authority and ordain thee to this office, that thou mayst have power to expound the Scriptures, and to bless, elevate and strengthen thy sisters. The Lord is well pleased with thee, with thy diligence, fidelity, and zeal in the interest of thy sisters. He has blessed thee exceedingly, and will continue to bless thee forever and ever; and I bless thee with all thine heart can desire in righteousness, and seal upon thee all former blessings conferred upon thee by the Holy Priesthood, in the name of Jesus. Amen."

Record keeper that she was, Eliza R. Snow, who had been secretary of the original women's organization, had carried all the minutes and accounts, including Joseph Smith's detailed teachings, with her across the plains. So when Brigham Young called on her to reorganize the Female Relief Society, she was well prepared to do so. Following Joseph's directions exactly, and certainly with Brigham's approval, Eliza set about her task with alacrity.

With counselors Zina D. H. Young and Elizabeth Ann Whitney, both capable and both good friends, she began to visit all the wards in the city and in outlying settlements. Soon it became apparent that the task was too big for the three of them, so seven other leading women were assigned to assist in the church-wide organization. They traveled in every means of conveyance available, becoming "experts at repairing wagon wheels and buggy tongues, and they were quick and skillful in harnessing and unharnessing the teams, which often they were obliged to do when help was not available." By 1868, branches of the Relief Society had been installed in all 20 wards in Salt Lake City plus nearly every outlying community.

Organizing new branches comprised only a small part of Eliza's overall responsibility as president of the women's groups. Special callings and assignments were frequently made by Brigham Young which she, in turn, handed down to the various local leaders. The assignments were varied, all based on the needs of a frontier people.

Few medical doctors existed among the Mormons. One of the first assignments Eliza received was to institute a nursing program, to ensure that at least three women in each Relief Society branch were knowledgeable in hygiene and nursing. Ultimately women would be sent to medical schools to become certified physicians. The worthwhile endeavor to provide adequate medical care for all the Saints culminated in 1882 with the establishment of the Deseret Hospital.

Eliza spent many taxing years raising money for the facility.

That the hospital was a strain on Eliza is evident from her own words: "I realized the great need and import of the movement, and did not feel to shrink from my labor or responsibility, but when my time was all occupied, as it truly was at that time; for me to involve myself in other and untried duties, seemed nothing short of subscribing to neglect of those already resting upon me: but I obtained a promise that after the hospital was in good running order, I might resign."

As president of the board of directors, Eliza spent a great deal of time consulting, planning, and meeting with the other board members, but her efforts were successful. She felt a great deal of personal satisfaction to "extend relief to suffering humanity." Eliza and the other board members received no pay for their work. "But one remuneration," she wrote, "consisted in the consciousness of doing our duty."

At Brigham's request, Eliza also led the women in a home production movement. Brigham "urged upon them the manufacture of articles made of straw—the cultivation of silk, and the establishment of fashions that would be becoming—such as would be worthy of the patronage of sensible, refined and intelligent women who stand as we in reality do, at the head of the world." Mormon women refined their artistic abilities and became skilled craftspeople. So well made were their articles that in 1876 Eliza endeavored to secure space at the United States Centennial Exhibit at Philadelphia. Because no exhibition space was available, she undertook the monumental task of organizing a local Women's Centennial Fair which was housed in the Old Constitution Building on Main Street in Salt Lake City. For eight weeks the ladies displayed their works of art to an abundant crowd.

The *Woman's Exponent* reported that, in part, the exhibition consisted of: "Very elegant and artistic specimens of wax fruit and flowers, artificial flowers for trimmings of all varieties and shades, almost innumerable varieties of ornamental and useful articles, for adding to the beauty and comfort of home. . . . One of the chief features of the fair is the silk worm in all its various forms and stages of production, from the egg to the cocoon, and from them to the article reeled, spun and woven.

"Competent judges of manufactured lace, assert the pillow, Ecru and Honiton lace on exhibition there, . . . [are] equal in worth to [that] manufactured elsewhere."

Because the home-manufactured goods were so well received at the centennial exhibition, Brigham asked Eliza to open a store where the women's crafts could be sold. Eliza herself acted as manager of the Woman's Commission House. The small handicraft store became a forerunner of a large-scale mercantile operation known as the Woman's Cooperative Store and Exchange.

As Brigham called Eliza to take responsibility for the much more involved venture, he remarked in his outspoken manner, "The women can take hold and do all of the trading for these wards as well as to keep a big loafer to do it. It is always disgusting to me to see a big fellow handing out calicoes and measuring ribbon. I would rather see the ladies do it. Let them do this business and let the men go to raising sheep, wheat, or cattle."

Eliza was considered a fragile woman. But she was fragile only in outward appearance. She worked long full days supervising the cooperative store, and she proved to be an exacting businesswoman. One day an incident occurred when one of Brigham Young's mill managers hotly disputed a pre-arranged commission on fabric. Eliza minced no words in the note she immediately dispatched to Brigham Young:

"Dear President Young,

"...Although we are novices in the mercantile business, we are not green enough for that kind of management."

She signed her note, "With love, Eliza R. Snow."

Not all of Eliza's duties originated with Brigham Young. At times other individuals came forward with good ideas. But, no matter what the source of the suggestion, Eliza soon became the organizer of the project. The origin of the *Woman's Exponent*, the first newspaper in the church directed to women, was a case in point.

Louisa Green was an aspiring young writer who felt a kinship with Eliza. In fact, being a great-niece to Brigham Young, Louisa called her "Aunt Eliza," as did many of Brigham's children and relatives. Louisa had contributed a number of articles and poems to the *Salt Lake Herald* and was considered by the editor, Edward L. Sloan, to possess considerable writing ability. Sloan was enough impressed with Louisa's work to offer her the position of editor for a women's newspaper he hoped to publish. Louisa certainly felt complimented by the offer, but at first she refused. Sloan wrote again and told her "that it was her work that inspired the idea of such a paper and that if she further declined, the idea of a woman's paper would be abandoned."

Being a young woman and not entirely confident that she was equal to the job, Louisa Green replied that if the project were approved by Eliza R. Snow and if Brigham Young would *call* her to be the editor of the paper, she would accept the call.

Brigham Young, enthusiastically agreeing that the women needed a forum for their expression, placed the organization of the *Woman's Exponent* under the direction of the Relief Society, squarely on Eliza's shoulders. And Louisa Green did indeed become the first editor.

The Mormon ladies, and especially Eliza, relished the boast that their newspaper was a rarity in the entire Christian world at that time. A semi-monthly journal, the paper was thoroughly Mormon in content, its material much appreciated by the women in the city as well as those living in outlying areas where it offered their most current source of information. The female contributors, plus the regular staff, offered articles detailing their local Relief Society activities, poetry filled with flowery phrases, notices of births, deaths and weddings, and news of coming events pertaining to women.

Only fragmentary evidence exists to suggest Eliza's involvement in selecting staff members and contributors to the paper. But of course she knew the ladies in the valley who showed the most talent for writing. Among those selected from time to time were Lu. Dalton, Emily Woodmansee and Hannah King. From England, Hannah seemed to have a gift for expressing the queen's language.

Most of the prominent contributors promoted with exhaustive zeal the duties of women in the political and organizational affairs of the territory. The issue of women's suffrage claimed a good deal of space. Of course it was fashionable for writers to have a *nom de plume*; Sarah Russell had hers—"Hope." Teachers, most of them, the contributors lent to the paper a marked tone of sobriety and formality, making the *Woman's Exponent*, by today's standards, deadly dull. Common journalistic practice at that time avoided specifics in retelling an incident that was newsworthy. The style of the day seemed to be to relate the incident in the most ethereal generalities, so of course no one would be offended. Even Louisa Green and later Emmeline B. Wells, as editors, avoided specific criticism in the editorial section.

For all the provincialism exhibited by the newspaper, though, Eliza's position as its president offered her a ready source of publication for any and all materials she personally wished to publish. It was unthinkable that a staff member would reject *anything* submitted by Eliza R. Snow. To be sure, they all but worshipped her. Every year on January 21st, a large birthday tribute to Eliza would appear. In fact, in nearly every edition, some article or poem in praise of Eliza was printed.

The semi-monthly newspaper was finally replaced by a small monthly magazine, entitled very practically, *The Relief Society Magazine*. Nonetheless, the *Woman's Exponent* faithfully served the women of the Relief Society for 42 years, its last publication on February 14, 1914.

Eliza R. Snow has sometimes been judged as being void of that spark of imagination which allows a mind to create, to originate, to come forward with fresh ideas. It is true that her greatest talent as a leader lay in organization, after someone else had initiated a plan. But where young ladies were concerned, her absolute opinions gave birth to some powerful, fresh ideas. And one of Eliza's opinions was that the young women she observed were far too frivolous.

In many ways, Eliza was an enigma, nowhere so clearly as in her dress. Clarissa Young Spencer wrote of her Aunt Eliza, "She was very extravagant in her own mode of dress, invariably putting yards and yards of material into her skirts and trimming her gowns as elaborately as possible, but she could not bear to see a like extravagance in the younger generation, her feelings on the subject, indeed, amounting almost to fanaticism. I haven't the least doubt but what she was entirely sincere in the matter, evidently believing that what was quite all right for a woman of her judgment and experience would fill the heads of the young girls with vain and idle thoughts."

Clarissa told of the time her father presented each of the older girls with a wide grosgrain ribbon sash. How excited they were! One of the girls, Phoebe, laid her sash out on her bed with a party dress, all ready to wear that evening to a dance. When she returned to her room after dinner, however, the sash had disappeared. Apparently Eliza had already voiced some of her austere opinions, because Phoebe burst into angry tears, declaring to her mother that she was *sure* that Aunt Eliza had taken it. Unwilling to listen as her mother tried to calm her, Phoebe waylaid her father in the hall, unleashing the same accusation she had made to her mother. Clarissa described the scene as follows:

"'All right, daughter, we'll see,' Father replied mildly, and as Aunt Eliza came by on her way to the prayer room he stopped her and said, 'Phoebe has lost a sash. Have you seen anything of it?'

"'Yes, President Young,' she said. 'I felt that you wouldn't approve of anything so frivolous for your girls so I put it away.'

"'Sister Eliza,' said Father, 'I gave the girls those ribbons, and I am the judge of what is right and wrong for my girls to wear. Phoebe is to have her sash.'"

Eliza acquiesced to her husband's wishes for the time being, but Brigham soon began to see the wisdom behind Eliza's concerns for the young women of Zion. "The big ten," as his oldest bevy of girls was called, could sense the mood of their elders. In order to avoid even more criticism, they began to make a habit of loosening the waistbands of their tight skirts before joining the family in prayer, so that their bustles wouldn't appear so conspicuous.

But loosening waistbands was not what Aunt Eliza had in mind. Soon the Retrenchment Society, another of her full-steam-ahead projects, was a reality. Clarissa wrote:

"... but there came a time when Father called all of the girls into the parlor and announced that they were becoming entirely too adept in following the fashions of 'the world' and that he would like them to modify their manner of dress. Flounces were to be curtailed, bangs were no longer to be frizzed, bustles were to be subdued; in fact, they were to retrench in all the vanities and frivolities of the world and set an example for the rest of the daughters of Zion to follow."

A regular organization ensued, complete with officers and meetings. One of the Retrenchment Society's goals, in addition to encouraging the young women to be more modest and demure, was to establish a library of worthwhile reading materials suitable for young minds to absorb. This the members quickly accomplished. Soon, Eliza encouraged the brethren to organize the young men, under the direction of the priesthood. When this was effected, the two groups often joined together for parties and meetings, even sharing the library.

The Retrenchment Society has changed names as the times have changed, but it has endured through the years and is, even today, a fine source of education and social refinement for young Latter-day Saints all over the world.

Surely Eliza was satisfied. It was not the first time she had tried to alter the dress of Mormon women. During the 1850s, perhaps in an effort to ensure that even the poorest sisters could dress as well as the wealthier ladies, Eliza had tried to standardize women's dress in the Utah Territory. The result was the "Deseret Costume, a hideous affair consisting of bloomers and full skirts, without trimming, hoops, or trains." Not surprisingly, the style did not become popular.

It would be interesting to have read Eliza's thoughts as she sat painstakingly sewing lace and buttons to her own lovely dresses.

In August, 1878, after the death of Brigham Young, while waiting for a train in Farmington, a women named Aurelia Rogers, much concerned about the rough, careless ways many of the young men and boys had at the time, asked Eliza, "'What will our girls do for husbands, if this state of things continues? Could there not be an organization for little boys, and have them trained to make better men?'" With but an hour for discussion, Eliza and Aurelia, with the help of Emmeline Wells and a few other sisters, put together the skeletal plans for an organization for children ages four to twelve, to be extended to age sixteen in areas where there were few children.

After consulting the president of the church at that time, John Taylor, Eliza sought the local bishop's approval. That received, she wrote to Aurelia Rogers that Aurelia should consider herself authorized to proceed with a pilot program of the organization they named Primary.

The presiding brethren believed that the organization of a church-wide Primary would help produce fine citizens and leaders. So once more Eliza traveled up and down the territory with her faithful partner, Zina, speaking, encouraging, organizing, once holding more than 30 meetings in 15 days. An introduction given by the ward Relief Society in Kanab probably exemplified the general sentiments of all their audiences: "We welcome Sisters Eliza and Zina as our Eldest Lady and her Counselor, and as Presidents of all the feminine portion of the human race."

In spite of her strength as a leader, Eliza was a completely feminine woman. Just as she had coined the phrase "Eve's Tongue" for the pure Adamic language she used when speaking in tongues, she had a special title she preferred for her own position among her peers. Considering the monumental service she unstintingly gave, who could deny her the privilege of calling herself "Presidentess"?

Chapter Fourteen

As the Saints became more and more efficient in the organization of various auxiliaries within the framework of the church, Brigham Young began to consider broadening the scope of mission outreach activities. One possibility in particular, that of a monumental excursion to the Holy Land, had been discussed by the presiding brethren for some time. Eliza would play a critical part in it.

In 1842 Orson Hyde, with a great deal of sacrifice and hardship, had visited the great city of Jerusalem. He had personally dedicated the land at a stone altar on the Mount of Olives, pronouncing a blessing that from that time forth the nations of the earth would yield up Jews and assist them to their promised soil. However, the significance of that momentous occasion was clouded by the fact that Elder Hyde was all alone when he delivered the dedication. His assigned companion had not left New York as he had been called to do. President Young must have been concerned that no one had witnessed the singular historical event, for he devised a plan to send at least two of the leading brethren to rededicate the land to the return of the

Jews.

After much consideration, President Young determined which of the leading priesthood holders would best carry out the assignment to dedicate that ancient land. He named President George A. Smith, his first counselor in the First Presidency; Lorenzo Snow, and several others, including four women.

Years before, while crossing the plains, Eliza had received what she declared was a personal revelation, advising her that she would live to see the Holy Land. But when an invitation came to join the selected envoy to Palestine, she had quite forgotten the revelation. A friend to whom she had confided the experience came forward to remind her.

Eliza was the undisputed leader of all the Mormon sisters and because her demeanor was one of grace and dignity, it seems reasonable that she should have been chosen to represent the women of the church.

In a letter to President George A. Smith, who was a cousin to the Prophet Joseph and a man of sound financial sense, Brigham Young detailed the assignment, pointing out Smith's several duties and, by implication, those of Eliza and the others as well:

"15th October

"Dear Sir—As you are about to start on an extensive tour through Europe and Asia Minor, where you will doubtless be brought in contact with men of position and influence in society, we desire that you observe closely what openings now exist, or where they may be effected, for the introduction of the Gospel into the various countries you shall visit.

"When you get to the land of Palestine, we wish you to dedicate and consecrate that land to the Lord, that it may be blessed with fruitfulness, preparatory to the return of the Jews, in fulfillment of prophecy and the accomplishment of the purposes of our heavenly Father.

"We pray that you may be preserved to travel in peace and safety, that you may be abundantly blessed with words of wisdom and free utterance in all your conversations pertaining to the holy Gospel, dispelling prejudice and sowing seeds of righteousness among the people.

Signed Brigham Young
Daniel H. Wells.

On October 26, 1872, Eliza left Salt Lake's Lion House by train on the first leg of her trip. She was 68 years old. Her brother Lorenzo Snow joined her at Ogden, and together they sped to Chicago and on to New York to join their full party.

The rapid journey across the plains, once traversed so painfully, impressed Eliza like few things she had ever experienced. She had lived to see man attain speeds she never thought possible in her lifetime. In one of her frequent letters home she expressed what that experience meant to her, writing: "In crossing the plains, I frequently drew the contrast between the present and the past, and could hardly realize the present to be a living reality. To travel with ease, devoid of fatigue, in three days, a distance which a few years ago required more than three months of weariness and privation to accomplish, is certainly a very great change."

She looked out at the newly spanned bridge over the Missouri River and declared it "a piece of workmanship worthy of a critical daylight observation." After passing through a typical thunderstorm at Council Bluffs during the night, Eliza noted, "It was 9 o'clock at night, but what were the night and the storm to us! Instead of pitching tents and circling beneath a dripping roof, we were comfortably seated in a palace car and travelling at an almost incredible speed. So much for the blessings of God on the march of improvement."

In New York, Eliza and Lorenzo joined the other members of their party, making a group of nine in all. Some were on their way to European missions, others would journey on with Eliza and Lorenzo.

On November 6, 1872, they boarded the steam-powered sailing vessel *Minnesota* for the two-week voyage to England. Of that singular first crossing of the Atlantic aboard the swaying passenger ship, Eliza delicately recorded the following: "We have had considerable rough weather, but now it is calm. I have experienced a slight touch of that disquieting malady called seasickness, just enough to make my appetite inexpensive for two or three days, and to cause a little cleansing of the stomach for my future benefit." But with all of her discomfort, Eliza fared better than some of the others. An interesting letter to the *Salt Lake Herald* from Paul A. Schettler described the scene:

"President George A. Smith had a pretty hard time of it, as he [being overweight] could hardly turn over in his berth; but with the rest of us the contrary was the case, as we were continually rolled from one side to the other, and had to brace ourselves against some part of the berth to prevent our being pitched out. Miss E. R. Snow has stood the voyage and sea-sickness so far, as well as any of us, and has given us a good deal of intellectual enjoyment."

At length the *Minnesota* crossed the Atlantic and arrived in Liverpool on schedule. After two days in the mighty port city, the party took a train to London. Eliza formed some strong opinions of London. She wrote, "Stopped nine days in that mamoth [sic] city of world-wide interest, and withal, so unsystematically planned, that when asked how I liked London, I invariably replied, that, were I to shape it to my liking, I should, in the first place, take it to pieces and straighten out its streets."

From England the group spent several weeks touring the European continent by rail, then traveled by steamer across the Mediterranean to Alexandria, Egypt. Eliza's spirits were high as she crossed the Mediterranean Sea. In a poem titled "Sunrise on the Mediterranean," one stanza reveals the lilt of her spirit:

> The sparkling waves of the sea below,
> The blazoning over head,
> The horizon wrapped in a burning glow,
> A thrilling enchantment spread.

Following a brief stay in Cairo to view the pyramids of that ancient region, the party sailed from Port Said to Palestine, arriving at the port of Jaffa. This was the city of Jonah's adventure, the city known as Joppa, their gateway to the Holy Land.

"On approaching Jaffa from the sea, it presents a charming and picturesque appearance, being situated upon a high eminence, its streets rising one above another like seats in an amphitheatre, surrounded by beautiful lemon and orange groves and tall waving cypresses." Lorenzo and the others had already learned the way of avoiding harassment by public officials: "On entering the custom house with our baggage," he said, "some francs bestowed upon the smiling, obsequious Mussulman official, saved the trouble of looking up our passports and occupying time which otherwise would have been employed by officious Turks in ransacking our satchels and trunks."

In 1872 Palestine was part of the old but declining Ottoman Empire, ruled as a colony by Turkey. Because that government had no advanced civilization to boast of, all its colonies were at least a century behind the western world in technology. For one thing, no railroads existed in Palestine. So at that point in the company's travels, the Saints resorted to horses and tents. Of that experience Lorenzo wrote that prearranged transportation had been set for the two-day trek inland to Jerusalem. As had been the case with their preceding modes of conveyance, the facilities were the finest they could secure. The travelers planned well for the entire sweep through Palestine to Lebanon. Among the items they assembled were: "two sleeping tents, a separate one for the ladies, a kitchen tent with cook stove, a saloon or dining tent, iron bedsteads, mattresses, clean white sheets, abundance of bedding, carpets and camp stools. We were provided with good horses, saddles, an efficient drago man, plenty of servants and preparations to serve three meals per day, under the supervision of an experienced cook."

That first day on the winding road to Jerusalem, a sense of expectation permeated the group. They were nearing the Holy City. The very fact that they were on the soil of the ancient Hebrews sent the party forward with reverent awe. Lorenzo mentioned in his letters, "We felt that we were passing over the land once occupied by the children of Abraham, the plains once trod by the kings of Israel with their marshaled hosts, the land of the Apostles and Prophets. We were in Palestine! The Holy Land! The consciousness of the fact was inspiring."

They spent that night camped in a basin, the hills leading up to Jerusalem in the distance. The following morning the Saints arose and after an early breakfast, with their "faces toward the 'Holy City,'" they moved forward. At noon they stopped in the shade of an olive tree near the spot where, according to tradition, David had selected stones with which to combat Goliath.

For an hour's ride following lunch the party ascended to the city of Jerusalem. They noticed first the city of David, then off to the left the barren Mount of Olives. "We slowly and thoughtfully wind our way down the hill, passing the Russian buildings and other prominent establishments, until we reach the city and enter our encampment."

The travelers spent the night, then toured the region for three days, visiting Solomon's Pools, Bethlehem, the convent of Mar Saba, the Dead Sea and the Jordan River, returning by way of Bethany to Jerusalem.

While on that three-day excursion they saw all the notable sights as well as fierce, armed Bedouins who were disarmed by the guides. As they returned to Jerusalem, Lorenzo explained in summary that, "as we approached Jerusalem, we descended a steep hill, down a rocky, winding, shelvy path, past an immense cemetery and the Garden of Gethsemane, with its ornamental trees, gravel walks, flowers and shrubbery, then around the towering battlements of Jerusalem, and soon reached our encampment, well pleased with our three days' excursion."

Within the Holy City, the group made the usual rounds of holy shrines: the Stone of Unction, the Holy Sepulchre, the Hill of Calvary. The guide made certain he pointed out the hole in which the cross had been planted, the marble on the exact spot where Christ was laid in the tomb. In the marketplace hawkers were everywhere, selling "sacred relics." After listening to the guide's countless references to this object being a piece of the cross or that object being the exact rock rolled away from the tomb, Eliza began to challenge him on the accuracy of his information. She had endured enough, particularly from a guide who claimed to be "an archaeologist lecturer, etc." When he conducted the Mormon group to the "Holy Staircase" and said it was the identical one that the Savior had ascended in the court of Pilate, Eliza asked the guide if he would swear to it.

He replied, emphatically, "I will swear to the aquaduct, and I will swear to the Arch of Titus." Those objects stood in front of them.

She had made her point. One can imagine the guide winking at Eliza, to let her know his pitch was all a tourist game. But she had no patience with such triflings.

Eliza expressed in writing her impressions of the guided tours that stretched her credulity. Observing that even though she took little of the guide's words as truth, she felt that the Saints "were really where the ancient Jerusalem once stood, and consequently in the vicinity where those scenes transpired, and it did not matter essentially whether Mary stood on this or that side

126

of the sepulchre when Jesus manifested himself to her after his resurrection, whether the one secured in the wall, which we were permitted to touch with a rod, was the 'True Cross,' etc., etc. We know by incontrovertible testimony, that here Jesus was crucified for the redemption of man, was resurrected, ascended, and, at no very distant day, 'will in like manner descend.'"

Except for those first few hours at sea when the group steamed out of New York, Eliza never complained of illness of any kind. That is remarkable, considering the variety of food and poor sanitation she was subjected to throughout the Near East. But the Mormons had been careful to eat, sleep and toilet at their own encampment. In that way they were not as likely to contract the germs that surely must have flourished in the local hotels and eating places.

Eliza frequently expressed her good health and high spirits: "We were all in good spirits; my health was never better, although 'sight seeing' is not the easiest work in the world."

On March 2, 1872, President Smith made arrangements with his dragomen to carry a tent, table, seats and carpet up to the Mount of Olives for a special service. The Saints rode by horseback to the spot for the dedication after taking time to visit the Church of Ascension, a small cathedral that once again some claimed to be the spot where Christ ascended into heaven.

Of that occasion, Eliza wrote, "By the time the tent was prepared, which we entered, and after an opening prayer by Brother Carrington, we united in service in the order of the Holy Priesthood, President Smith leading in humble, fervent supplication, dedicating the land of Palestine for the gathering of the Jews and the rebuilding of Jerusalem, and returning heartfelt thanks and gratitude to God for the fulness of the Gospel and blessing bestowed on the Latter-day Saints ... to me it seemed the crowning point of the whole tour, realizing as I did that we were worshipping on the summit of the sacred Mount, once the frequent resort of the Prince of Life."

Finally leaving Jerusalem and heading to Beirut on horseback, the Mormon party rode through Samaria to Nazareth and on to the Sea of Galilee. At the shores of Galilee, half of the party decided to traverse the River Jordan and row across the 15-mile-wide Sea of Galilee by boat. Eliza, Lorenzo and others rode on horseback along the shore instead, but eventually the two parties would reunite at the far end of the sea at an encampment.

Along the shore, because Eliza's group was in advance of the boat party, she took time to soak in the inspiration that famous lake had to offer.

It was mid-March and, according to Lorenzo, as they stood in the spring sun there was a "remarkable clearness of the atmosphere." Eliza gathered shells as she picked her way along the shore, very much aware of the influence of the Savior on that same shore. She wrote in verse her feelings as she looked out on the water:

> I have stood on the shore of the beautiful sea,
> The renown'd and immortalized Galilee,
> When 'twas wrapp'd in repose at eventide,
> Like a royal queen in her regal pride.
>
> I thought of the present—the past; it seem'd
> That the silent sea with instruction teem'd;
> For often, indeed, the heart can hear
> What never, in sound, has approached the ear.
>
> There's a depth in the soul, that's beyond the reach
> Of all earthly sound—of all human speech,
> A fiber too sacred and pure to chime
> With the cold, dull music of Earth and Times.
>
> Again when the shades of night, were gone,
> In the clear bright rays of the morning dawn,
> I walked on the bank of this self-same Sea,
> Where once our Redeemer was wont to be.

Eliza's step must have been light as she strolled along the seashore. The spirit of near gloom that had enveloped her while walking through the city of Jerusalem and winding her way along the narrow passageways of numerous villages, lifted like heavy grey fog as Eliza refreshed herself at the Sea of Galilee. Near the end of her walk, a young Jewess handed Eliza a bunch of hyssop and asked her if she would care to visit the woman's home and meet her mother. Eliza was pleased to do so.

When the travelers left the famous Sea of Galilee, they wound their way northeast to the trail at the base of Mount Hermon and ascended 5,000 feet through rough passes and trails where strewn rocks were smooth as glass. At the upper plains leading to the ancient city of Damascus, Eliza wrote, "The way was lined on each side with grape vines, seemingly well cultivated." The beautiful scenery shaped by industrious farmers and skilled orchardists caught Eliza's interest. Not since the Saints had left Europe had Eliza seen such evidence of hard work. The inhabitants met with Eliza's approval, unlike the Bedouin tribes that they had encountered from Jaffa to Damascus, who troubled Eliza. She and her brother referred to those people as "degenerated."

Damascus seemed to Eliza to be truly "the Pearl of the East." Lorenzo described it best: "Its wide extended plains, on which are a hundred villages, numerous mosques looming up here and there, above the immense, spreading mass of broad, white roofs, their great swelling domes and tapering minarets adorned with golden crescents, the great plain of Damascus, ornamented with rich fields and beautiful gardens, groves of poplar and walnut, orchards of figs, apricots and pomagranates and numerous vineyards sprinkled here and there . . . stretching east far away till lost beneath the gray horizon northward . . . where it is bounded by the river Pharpar, of Scripture memory."

The American opinion that Mormon women were being "held in a state of vassalage" never took hold in the Near East. As a matter of fact, at Damascus a shimmering light of approval grew as the people learned of the Mormons' belief. When the consular agent there inquired about the Mormons' faith, George A. Smith responded that the Mormons believed in the patriarchal order of marriage. In turn, the agent replied that the Muslims of Damascus could marry four wives and buy as many as they pleased. He informed the Mormon group that the Turks would not allow women to vote as the Mormons did, because to do so would be placing them too nearly equal with men.

Between visits to the officials of the city and conversations with visitors to their encampment, the whole experience at Damascus seemed highly rewarding. When a group of Damascus women learned that a group of Saints had camped by the city and that there were western women on the tour, an assembly of 400 Muslim women came en masse to visit Eliza and Clara Little. The friendly sight of so many curious, veiled ladies intrigued Eliza, and she entertained them as graciously as one in a tent could do.

The travelers found the culture and lifestyle of the Mediterranean people vastly different from that of their homeland. They missed the simple ordinances which would have regulated animal control and disposal of garbage. They found the most annoying negligence to involve the hundreds of mongrel dogs which were allowed to run free, traveling in packs about the city and its surrounding villages.

Done at Damascus, Eliza and her group started on the broad road through the mountains to the sea at Beirut. They left the entire area "without shedding any tears of regret."

By March 25, 1873, the Mormon tourists stood at the docks of Beirut eager to steam for home. They would yet visit many famous cities—Constantinople, Athens, and a host of European cities—as part of their itinerary along the route home.

The *Woman's Exponent* summarized the Holy Land travels of Eliza best when it reported: "On the 25th embarked on the Steamer *Mars*, of the Austrian Lloyd line, *enroute* for Constantinople. Sister Eliza had been, at her somewhat advanced time in life, enduring 'twenty-nine days of tent life, and twenty-one riding on horseback.' While remembering she was in her seventieth year, one cannot help thinking she was a woman of fortitude and remarkable powers of endurance." Eliza's 69th birthday had been celebrated while traveling, thus the reference to her 70th year.

The greatest and perhaps most pleasing side effect of travel to and from the Near East was Eliza's and Lorenzo's stopoff in Kansas City, where they met with their youngest brother, Samuel Snow, 17 years younger than Eliza. It had been more than 20 years since they had last seen each other.

Samuel had done very well. He had a large family and a half section of rich farmland which impressed the elder brother and sister greatly.

Besides visiting Samuel, Eliza and Lorenzo also met with old friends and some relatives in Ohio. Of that visit Eliza wrote, "Very many of our relatives and friends have 'gone the way of all the earth' since we left, and everything of remembrance has yielded to the strokes of the battle axe of changeful times."

> Our former loved associates
> Have mostly passed away;
> While those we knew as children
> Are crowned with locks of gray.

* * *

And thus, as in a mirror's
Reflection, we are told.
With stereotyped impressions
The fact of growing old.

Those impressions of age seemed to settle on Eliza's mind to remind her she had much to do and little time in which to do it.

Even though both she and Lorenzo were anxious to get home, they prolonged those visits in the Midwest, making the most of every possible moment. "Being desirous of seeing as many of our friends and relatives as possible," Eliza wrote, "we visited night and day, going from place to place in rapid succession. I am inclined to think that so much visiting was never before done in so little time."

Eliza and Lorenzo not only renewed family ties, but they also gathered genealogies of both the living and the dead. It was a most satisfying trip.

Eliza took the train from Ogden to Salt Lake City after kissing her brother goodbye as he parted to return north to his home in Brigham City. On the warm summer evening when Eliza slipped back into the Lion House, no one at the station or on the streets noticed her return. She quietly embraced her family inside the Youngs' compound. Had the committee been notified, they would have welcomed her home with brass band and flags flying. Instead, the first public notice of her return came in the daily paper:

"So carefully and silently was the closing portion of the return trip of Eliza R. Snow concluded, that not until Thursday, the fourth day after her arrival, when the return of her brother, President Lorenzo Snow, to Brigham City, was noticed in the daily papers, was it suspected by many of her friends that she was again safe at home in this city..."

Eliza had been away from home for fully nine months. In a salutation to the ladies of Utah, given on July 14, 1873, Eliza wrote: "Thanks, my dear Sisters, for your faith and prayers, through which, in a great measure, I attribute the blessings of God in the wonderful prosperity which, from first to last, attended the party of tourists of which I have the honor of having been a member. We have traveled twelve thousand miles by water, and nearly or quite thirteen thousand by land, without accident, and without a single failure in making connection, either with steamer or railroad; and are now safely home.

"Here let me beg acceptance of my thanks, and acknowledgment of my appreciation of the kind and generous feelings that prompted arrangements for my reception, which I very innocently frustrated by a quiet arrival."

Those generous sisters had not only planned a gala reception in her honor, but had together raised the money to finance Eliza's portion of the excursion. And now she was home, to continue her service to them as the Relief Society president.

Eliza—Superior Mind, Tender Soul

Chapter Fifteen

How good it was to be back in Zion among her sisters! Eliza basked in their love. More invitations to speak were extended than she could humanly accept. But she did her best, departing on a whirlwind tour to speak to as many branches of the Relief Society as possible. She must have felt that all who had contributed to her grand tour deserved a report.

Certainly one topic Eliza addressed was her recent visit to the Holy Land. But she was a teacher; a mere travelogue would have seemed to her a waste of time, both for the audience and the speaker. So naturally she instructed and exhorted.

Through the years Eliza had developed some interesting theories to explain or define certain points of church doctrine. She had absorbed every word the Prophet Joseph ever spoke in her presence, as well as those of other noted church orators, Parley and Orson Pratt, John Taylor and Heber C. Kimball among her favorites. She had also listened to Brigham Young's mini-lectures daily for more than 25 years. It is little wonder that as her confidence and stature grew, she began not only to form opinions of her own, but to expound on them from the pulpits of numerous wards as well.

After all, had she not received resounding approval for the wondrous new doctrine in her hymn, "O My Father"? And had she not been given positions of heady responsibility over and over again? Did not her husband, Brigham Young, regard her opinion to be as valuable as those of the leading brethren? And was she not the leader of all the women in the church, not only in religious matters, but in political concerns as well? Eliza had been the keynote speaker at dozens of women's meetings, arousing their support for women's suffrage with her stirring words.

So Eliza, in her unassuming but dignified manner, began to express her own interpretation of some specific church teachings. One of the doctrinal points she raised was prompted by the concern for Mormon women voiced by national women's suffrage speakers. These speakers portrayed the polygamous Mormon wives as yoked in bondage, and pleaded with them to unite and rise up against their vile and lecherous husbands.

In spite of the fact that Eliza had found the doctrine of polygamy repugnant when it was first presented to her, she had prayed and studied until she felt that she had been divinely enlightened on the subject.

Eliza was keenly perceptive as she pondered words of the Lord to Moses in the *Pearl of Great Price* regarding the formation of the world and the fall of man. She believed and taught that before the fall, Adam and Eve were more than equal, they were one, male and female, each a part of the other, addressed as one. Because Eve was the first to hearken unto the voice of Satan, she was placed in a subservient position: ". . . thy desire shall be to thy husband and he shall rule over thee," the Lord commanded Eve. Eliza seized her speaking opportunities to expand her personal insights into an interpretation of the decision of Eve.

In an address given to the Female Relief Society of Weber County, Utah, in the 1870s, Eliza taught that only by partaking of the new and everlasting covenant of eternal marriage could that once perfect team, male and female, again be welded into one. By complete obedience to all of God's commandments and by being married—that is, sealed for time and eternity—to a righteous man, a woman could elevate herself from her subservient level back to an equal position with her husband. In no other way could this be done.

Thus Eliza not only accepted polygamy but joyfully embraced it, even promoted it as the solution to all of women's woes.

Always it seemed to her that the righteous women of the church far outnumbered the righteous men. Thus, according to Eliza, only through commitment to the doctrine of plural marriage, in which many worthy women could all be sealed to one worthy man, could every pure woman receive the opportunity to redeem herself before her God.

Defending herself and her sisters before the pity of the suffragettes, Eliza asked in the tabernacle before a large assembly, "Do you know of any place on the face of the earth, where woman has more liberty, and where she enjoys such high and glorious privileges as she does here as a Latter-day Saint?"

Eliza and her husband almost always saw things in the same way. One amusing exception depicts Eliza's firm belief that, no matter how painful, woman must, at least in this life, bend her will to that of man.

In pondering the doctrine of literal resurrection, Eliza was not content until mentally she could make the whole process fit together logically. It bothered her intensely that she was expected to believe that the same bodies that decompose and become elements of soil—and subsequently of plants which are eaten by animals, which in turn may be eaten by other animals, in an endless round of existence from generation to generation—could possibly be sorted out and each being receive, in the resurrection, only the elements which originally and uniquely were part of that being. It could not be so, Eliza was sure. She could not content herself with the pat answer, "With God, all things are possible."

In a long, scientifically presented article in the *Woman's Exponent*, Eliza set forth a logical alternative explanation that she may have heard from Orson Pratt. To most subscribers, it was a brand new doctrine. Eliza titled her piece, "Mortal and Immortal Elements of the Human Body," with a subtitle: "A Philosophical Objection To The Resurrection, Removed." After using two columns of the *Woman's Exponent* to state her reasons for disbelief in the long-accepted church position on the subject, Eliza proceeded to give what she thought was an inspired solution.

"But thanks to God for the key which solves the mystery," she wrote. "Every organized human body independent of the spirit (which is a separate organization) is composed of two distinct grades or classes of matter, and in such mutual combination as to serve the purposes of this lower existence. One is gross, volatile, subject to change and decay through a precarious union of earth, air, fire and water—tangible to mortal sight and touch and subject to all the laws of decomposition. The other is pure, invisible, intangible and capable of resisting every law of infraction or dissolubility. This, when the spirit leaves the body, remains INTACT—never being incorporated with other bodies or substances. This is the precious material that will be resurrected in perfect form, and compose the immortal tabernacle of the immortal spirit.

"It is well understood that resurrected beings are invisible to these gross organs of sight except when they are quickened by immortal vision, that if the dead were brought within viewing distance of us we should not see them. Why not? The resurrected body, being composed of this pure material can only be seen by organs of sight formed by the same pure matter, unclogged with gross substances."

As might well be imagined, Eliza's philosophy was met by keen interest on all sides, so much so that the article was reprinted some time later by popular demand. In the very next issue after the reprinting took place, the following notice appeared prominently in the *Woman's Exponent* from Eliza's husband.

"Editor Woman's Exponent:

"In your issue of Sept. first, I notice an article written by Miss E. R. Snow, entitled 'Mortal and Immortal Elements of the Human Body,' republished from No. 13, Vol. 2, of your journal. The cause assigned for its reproduction in your paper is, that 'Saints and strangers were so interested' in its statements, and it had been so often called for that republication was decided upon.

"I sincerely regret that this demand should have arisen, I had hoped that after its first publication it would have slept and never been awakened; but the fact of its having been so repeatedly called for, places me under obligation to correct the minds of the Latter-day Saints in relation to the doctrine contained therein.

"On some future occasion when I have time I may possibly take up the article in detail, but at present shall simply say, as the prophet Joseph Smith once told an Elder who asked his opinion of a, so called revelation he had written,—'It has just one fault and that fault is, it is not true.'

> Brigham Young
> President of the Church of
> Jesus Christ of Latter-day Saints."

The same day that Brigham's disclaimer ran, a long, carefully composed article refuting Eliza's theory, point by point, was submitted by John Taylor and printed in the paper. But not a word was heard from Eliza.

Not until seven months later, in April, 1876, in a small, obscure box in the *Woman's Exponent* do we read:

"To whom it may concern. It will be recollected that an article written by me, entitled 'Mortal and Immortal Elements of the Human Body—A Philosophical Objection to the Resurrection Removed,' was published in the Woman's Exponent in September, 1875, and that subsequently an article written and signed by Pres. Young appeared in the Woman's Exponent in which the former was pronounced untrue.

"Permit me to say that I fully concur in the views expressed by Pres. Young, and withdraw everything contained in my article at variance therewith, and trust that no Latter-day Saint may be led into erroneous doctrine through anything written by me.

> Salt Lake City, March 19, 1876
> Eliza R. Snow."

Imagination feeds conjecture; perhaps it will never be known what words flew between the president and the presidentess. Perhaps words were a long time coming, surfacing only after cold silences had been mellowed by time. And suppose Eliza had written her philosophy in verse—would the clash have occurred at all? Whatever the scene, it is clear that Eliza humbled herself and acquiesced to the views of the priesthood, no small sacrifice considering the mind and will of Eliza R. Snow.

What must have been, at least, an embarrassment seems not to have affected Eliza's popularity or her role as leader at all. She continued to state her opinions with confidence.

Another fascinating doctrine Eliza espoused, not commonly fostered in contemporary teachings, was the "Adam-God" theory. One of Eliza's peers and admirers, Edward W. Tullidge, published a book titled *The Women of Mormondom* in 1877, and in it that theory was elaborated. A rambling hodge-podge of flowery praises for an assortment of women who had been spiritually valiant, the book was edited, strange as it may seem, by Eliza R. Snow. A number of pages were devoted worshipfully by Tullidge to her life, and certain sections were even written whole-cloth by Eliza herself. Thus we assume that Eliza agreed with the doctrine presented within the book.

Tullidge's version of the Adam-God position was that "Adam is the great archangel of this creation. He is Michael. He is the Ancient of Days. He is the father of our elder brother, Jesus Christ—the father of him who shall also come as Messiah to reign. He is the father of the spirits as well as the tabernacles of the sons and daughters of man. Adam!

"When this earth was prepared for mankind, Michael, as Adam, came down. He brought with him one of his wives, and he called her name Eve.

"The grand patriarchal economy, with Adam, as a resurrected being, who brought his wife Eve from another world, has been very finely elaborated, by Brigham, from the patriarchal genesis which Joseph conceived."

Current doctrinarians of the church, such as Elder Bruce R. McConkie, insist that Brigham Young's words have been totally misinterpreted by Tullidge and others unfriendly to the church. Elder McConkie states in his book, *Mormon Doctrine*: "Faithful members of the Church worship the Father, in the name of the Son, by the power of the Holy Spirit, and view Adam in his proper high place as the pre-existent Michael, the first man and presiding high priest (under Christ) over all the earth for all time..."

It is interesting to note, however, that Eliza said in a speech before the Sugar House Relief Society in 1868, "We should improve our talents for the time will come when every faithful man and woman will go forth like Adam and Eve."

A bit more light may be shed on both Brigham's and Eliza's view of the doctrine by Suza Young Gates, one of Brigham Young's daughters, in her book, *The Life Story of Brigham Young*. She wrote, "After prayers that evening he [Brigham Young] sat in council with Aunt Eliza R. Snow in the prayer-room. Edward Tullidge had compiled a story on the Women of Mormondom, which contained some interesting biography of the leading women of the Church and an account of the heroic struggle of those early years. Aunt Eliza and some of her associates thought it might be proper and advisable to send a group of women out into the world to give lectures on Mormonism and to dispose of the woman's book. Two of the daughters of Brigham Young were included in the list of women who were to go.

"'It is an experiment—but one I would like to see tried,'" said Brigham Young to Sister Snow at the close of the discussion. His untimely death, however, prevented the lecture tour from taking place. The ladies did not, in fact, venture out into the world to promote Tullidge's book. Presumably, however, Brigham Young, and certainly Eliza, had read and approved it.

Eliza continued to encourage her sisters to perform ordinances which are presently reserved for male priesthood holders only. On September 15, 1884, the year Eliza celebrated her 80th birthday, an article was printed in the *Woman's Exponent* in which selected questions, submitted by women throughout the church, were answered by their loftiest mentor, Eliza R. Snow.

Her reply to one question indicates the authority enjoyed by women as she perceived it. Eliza was asked, "Is it necessary for sisters to be set apart to officiate in the sacred ordinances of washing, anointing, and laying on of hands in administering to the sick?" Eliza answered, "It certainly is not. Any and all sisters who honor their holy endowments, not only have the right, but should feel it a duty, whenever called upon to administer to our sisters in these ordinances, which God has graciously committed to His daughters as well as to his sons; and we testify that when administered and received in faith and humility, they are accompanied with all-mighty power."

Through the years, Eliza increased her stature with the sisters, acknowledged not only as leader and teacher—encouraging them to use their divinely given powers to heal through faith—but accepted as a prophetic spokesperson as well.

In light of her many experiences, prophetically blessing others in the Adamic language, Eliza called herself not only poetess and presidentess, but "prophetess" as well. It is true that historians have agreed that only about half of her predictions came to pass, but those prophecies which *were* fulfilled were so publicized that she was considered a highly favored woman.

Heber J. Grant, who in later years became the president of the church, told a convincing story about Eliza's powers. He remembered playing on the floor at the feet of "Aunt Em" (Emmeline) Wells, Zina Young, Eliza R. Snow and others while they blessed one another in tongues. When they finished, Heber said that Eliza turned to him and "pronounced a blessing on my head by the gift of tongues, and Zina D. Young gave the interpretation." Heber understood very little and was astonished that Sister Snow was talking and pointing to him. All he remembered of the interpretation was that she said he would be a big man, and Heber thought she meant that he would grow tall.

But Heber's mother made a record of the blessing and referred to it frequently as Heber grew up, admonishing him, as he recalled, "If I would behave myself that honor would come to me." Heber laughed at her at the time, but later when as a young father he was ill, even close to death, priesthood holders administered to him, and Eliza's blessing was reaffirmed. Heber recovered, went on to be ordained an apostle and ultimately became president of the church.

In a discourse he gave in the Salt Lake Tabernacle, September 21, 1919, President Grant declared with emotion, "Tell me that the gift of tongues is not exercised in this Church? As well tell me that I do not know that I stand here today."

Eliza continued to speak and bless in tongues well into her 80s. At a conference, late in her life, she said: "This is a great work and the Gospel was designed to draw all people together. In the world, we thought the days of our youth was the time for happiness and enjoyment. I can bear my testimony to my young sisters that the older I grow the happier I am."

She had been widowed a second time in 1878, when Brigham Young, that great power behind her effectiveness, passed away. Eliza's last known recorded conversation with her husband had taken place the evening she presented her enthusiastically conceived plan for a lecture tour to promote Edward Tullidge's new book. Brigham had affably agreed that it was a plan worth trying when picking up his candle he added: "I think now I shall go and take my rest."

Within a week he was dead, the victim of a sudden attack of

"cholera morbus," which was thought later to have been appendicitis.

The splendid partnership of president and presidentess, prophet and prophetess had come to a halt. Though the team was disrupted, Eliza carried on alone for nearly a decade in her drive to enlighten and encourage the Saints.

Emmeline Wells, in a serialized article in the *Woman's Exponent*, wrote of Eliza's reaction to her husband's death thus:

"Sister Eliza although intimately associated in the family relation with Pres. Brigham Young and having resided under the same roof more than a quarter of a century, and assisted in various ways to promote his domestic happiness did not as many would have done, sit down and spend her time in mourning his death. She was too much interested in the work in which he had passed his lifetime, and seemed to renew her diligence if that were possible, in promoting the growth of all the organizations of women which existed in the Church."

Though she appeared frail and delicate—like a Dresden doll, as one niece described her—Eliza had, in actuality, a body as superior as her mind. She continued to draw on the reserves of both, long past the age when most people retire. Generations had passed—and still she continued to lead. But finally, inevitably, Eliza began to be old.

Chapter Sixteen

Eliza held no fear of death. Hers had been a life rich in experience and abundant in leadership fulfillment. If she sheltered any deep feelings of unfulfilled dreams, paramount must have been a desire to have had offspring. Her family had never been "bone of her bone and flesh of her flesh." It is only speculation that she regretted the void, because there is no evidence in her writings that she ever yearned for the crowning glory of motherhood. After all, she realized life was eternal and that surely she would yet be allowed that most rewarding experience.

Eliza knew as firmly as any of the several prophets she had conversed with that life would continue beyond the grave. At one point in her expressions on life and death Eliza wrote a work called "Immortality." It carried in its uplifting phrases a salute to life beyond the grave. Wrote Eliza:

> Yes Immortality: That bosom word,
> To me, has inspiration in it. Love
> Of life, is innate in human soul:
> 'Tis interwoven in our nature. 'Twas

Decreed in the grand council of the Gods,
When canvassing the great eternal scheme
Concerning destinies of man and earth;
That man should inherit love of life;
Else man, grown weary of a world of woes
And fickle tides of happiness, would haste
To make his exit, and e'en God Himself
Had fail'd to keep enough, as instruments,
On earth, to execute His purposes.

Several of Eliza's last poetic efforts revealed her anticipation of death, and correspondence among her friends traced the slow ebbing of her strength.

In a letter to a friend dated April 28, 1886, Emily P. Young wrote about Eliza's health: "I saw sister Eliza Snow this morning she is very feeble. A few weeks ago a large dog jumped upon her and threw her down and rolled and twisted her about and hurt her very bad and she was laid up seven weeks in consequence, and she says that she nor anybody else did not have much faith that she would ever get over it but she is better now, but she is very feeble yet. She is not able to see much company."

But 11 months later, Eliza's very good friend Emmeline B. Wells penned the following words to Mary E. Rollins Lightner: "Aunt Eliza is much improved in health since you were here and looks likely to live for years."

A month later in April, 1887, Emmeline told Mary: "Aunt Eliza is at present quite under the weather, in fact I do not think she has vitality enough to even give counsel, and ought not to be worried with anything. People do not seem to understand that she is delicate and needs lifting up, because her will power is so strong, she will not give way."

By June, even though most understood "Aunt Eliza" was "delicate," she had improved enough to go almost daily for buggy rides to visit old friends. She could walk about her apartment and, with help, step up into the carriage she used to get around town. But she never truly gained in health after the unfortunate incident with the dog.

Summer and fall came. At the onset of winter, at about ten o'clock on the morning of December 5, 1887, Patriarch John Smith, who had been a frequent caller and fellow companion on buggy rides, dropped by to see the frail Eliza. He went directly to her bedside in the Lion House apartment, where he spoke with her. The patriarch had undoubtedly been informed that Sister Snow was failing fast. He asked Eliza if she recognized him. "The customary smile lit up the beautiful countenance and the reply came in clear and distinct tones—'of course I do.' He blessed her, and she expressed her thankfulness."

Eliza had reflected on her pending death a mere two days before Patriarch Smith had pronounced that blessing. Speaking to several who sat at her bedside, she said, "I have no choice as to whether I shall die or live. I am perfectly willing to go or stay, as our Heavenly Father shall order. I am in His hands." One person present observed, "While she spoke, her wonderfully lustrous, dark eyes shone with more than earthly brightness, and as she conversed with those around her, the native intelligence which has so strongly individualized her, was remarkably exhibited, considering the weakness of her body."

Her brother, the apostle Lorenzo Snow, stood nearby; he had been in and out of the apartment for days. On December 5, he stayed on until afternoon when Eliza failed to respond to his voice, "and was by her side when she breathed her last."

At noon two days later, all the leading officials of Mormondom gathered at the Assembly Hall, that Gothic red-stoned church situated on the southwest corner of Temple Square. Pallbearers, followed by a long line of family members and dear friends, had conveyed Eliza's body from the Lion House in a neat casket of polished natural wood to the Assembly Hall.

When the casket entered the door, an overflow crowd of people who had loved and respected their "Aunt" Eliza rose to their feet.

Eliza had left instructions on the physical arrangement of the hall. She had requested and was granted white ribbons and draped white cloth instead of the customary black. Flowers, though difficult to get, were massed in profusion. The scene was bright and cheerful in the otherwise dark, stained-wood Assembly Hall.

Stake President Angus Cannon, who had been a youth at the time Joseph Smith, Jr., was assassinated, called the congregation to order. The choir sang, "I Know That My Redeemer Lives." After a prayer the choir sang Eliza's own immortal "O My Father," and for the remainder of the services a stream of church officials, among them John W. Taylor, A. O. Smoot and even the youthful Heber J. Grant, delivered tributes to Eliza. Most had been youngsters or were not yet born when Eliza crossed the plains to enter the valley of the Great Salt Lake. Actually, few in the large congregation were her contemporaries. Eliza had been the grand matriarch of the church for half a century. And though she had been an advocate of simple ceremony and quiet funerals, the Mormons who loved her desired to demonstrate their affection by crowding into the hall.

The outpouring of love and respect for one they deemed so noble and great seemed only appropriate for the occasion.

Following the benediction by Patriarch John Smith, members of the large congregation filed by to take one last look at the woman they honored as a true Saint. A funeral cortege followed the casket to the private cemetery that Brigham Young had established for his family. There Eliza's bishop, John R. Winder, directed while the young apostle Heber J. Grant dedicated the grave.

Praises to Eliza flooded the journals and newspapers. In particular, the tribute paid her in the *Deseret News* nearly a month after her death held a tone and quality of dignity, summarizing most of the adulations sung to her memory: "She has gone to mingle with the righteous who have kept the faith; to associate with her husband, the great Prophet of the last dispensation, to whom she has shown a sublime devotion that will be appreciated in the eternities to come... There was a marked harmony between the qualities of the heart and the gifts of the intellect of this remarkable woman... The purity of her life and nature necessarily rendered her a fit medium through whom the Holy Ghost could manifest those gifts and graces of the Gospel of the Redeemer that characterized the disciple of the Church of Christ... It may be said concerning her that she was indeed 'an elect lady.'"

A short time before her death, Eliza had penned a tender wish entitled, "My Epitaph."

> 'Tis not the tribute of a sigh
> From sorrow's heaving bosom drawn;
> Nor tears that flow from pity's eye,
> To weep for me when I am gone;

No costly balm, no rich perfume—
No vain sepulchral rite, I claim—
No mournful knell—no marble tomb—
No sculptur'd stone to tell my name.

A richer, holier tithe I crave,
Than time-proof monumental piers—
Than roses planted on my grave,
Or willows dripped in dewey tears.
The garlands of hypocrisy
May be equip'd with many a gem;
I prize the heart's sincerity
Above a princely diadem.

In friendship's memory let me live;
I know no selfish wish besides,
I ask no more; yet, O, forgive
This impulse of instinctive pride.
The silent pulse of memory
That beats to the unuttered tone
Of tenderness, is more to me
Than the insignia of a stone.

For friendship holds a secret cord,
That with the fibres of my heart
Entwines so deep, so close; 'tis hard
For death's dissecting hand to part,
I feel the low responses roll
Like far-off echoes of the night,
And whisper softly through my soul,
I would not be forgotten quite.

There was no question that Eliza touched the hearts of her contemporaries and the generations that followed after as few had ever done. Yet perhaps her greatest influence is felt through her verse, and not necessarily in those church organizations she helped to create, such as the Relief Society, Primary and Mutual. The words of her hymns touching sensitive souls live on: "O My Father," "How Great The Wisdom and The Love," "Behold The Great Redeemer Die" and "Though Deepening Trials," to name but a few, stand out among the best-loved hymns of the Latter-day Saints.

When eternities pass away and time is no more, Eliza Roxcy Snow shall not be forgotten, quite.

Sources Noted

Page

Chapter One

3 Edward W. Tullidge, *The Women of Mormondom.* New York: Tullidge and Crandall, 1877, p. 63.

4 Eliza R. Snow, "Sketch of My Life," in Nicholas G. Morgan's *Eliza R. Snow, An Immortal: Selected Writings of Eliza R. Snow.* Salt Lake City, Utah: Nicholas G. Morgan Sr. Foundation, 1957.

5 Ibid.

5 Tullidge, *Women of Mormondom*, p. 63.

5 Morgan, *Eliza R. Snow, An Immortal*, p. 5.

6 Ibid., p. 6.

6 *Western Courier*, Ravenna, Ohio, February 14, 1829.

6 Morgan, *Eliza R. Snow, An Immortal*, p. 6.

7 Ibid.

7 Tullidge, *Women of Mormondom*, p. 64.

7 Morgan, *Eliza R. Snow, An Immortal*, p. 6.

8 Ibid.

8 Ibid.

Page

9   Tullidge, *Women of Mormondom*, p. 69.
9   Morgan, *Eliza R. Snow, An Immortal*, p. 6.
10 Ivan J. Barrett, *Heroines of the Church*. Provo, Utah: Brigham Young University, 1973, p. 49.
10 Eliza R. Snow, *Biography and Family Record of Lorenzo Snow*. Salt Lake City, Utah: Deseret News Company, 1884, p. 5.
10 Ibid.
10 Ibid.

Chapter Two
11 Morgan, *Eliza R. Snow, An Immortal*, p. 1.
12 Ibid.
12 Ibid., p. 2.
12 Ibid.
12 Ibid.
13 Ibid., p. 3.
13 Some of the pen names used by Eliza R. Snow were Narcissa Pocahontas, Cornelia, Minerva, Tullia and A Mormon Girl.
14 Morgan, *Eliza R. Snow, An Immortal*, p. 4.
14 Snow, *Biography and Family Record*, p. 5.
15 Tullidge, *Women of Mormondom*, p. 84.
16 Ibid., pp. 94, 95.
16 *The Book of Mormon,* Moroni 10:8-17.
17 *Holy Bible,* King James Translation, 1 Corinthians 14:23, 26, 39, 40.
17 Carol Lynn Pearson, *Daughters of Light*. Provo, Utah: Trilogy Arts, 1973.

Chapter Three
19 Morgan, *Eliza R. Snow, An Immortal*, p. 7.
20 Ibid.
20 Ibid.
21 Snow, *Biography and Family Record*, p. 3.
21 Ibid.
21 Ibid., p. 4.
21 Ibid., p. 5.
21 Ibid., p. 6.
22 Ibid., p. 20.
23 Ibid., p. 21.

Page

23 Ibid.
23 Ibid., p. 22.
24 Ibid., p. 24.

Chapter Four
25 Ibid., p. 25.
26 Ibid., p. 26.
26 Ibid.
27 Ibid., p. 29.
28 Tullidge, *The Women of Mormondom*, p. 143.
28 Ibid.
28 Ibid., pp. 144, 145.
28 Ibid., p. 145.
29 Ibid., pp. 146, 147.
30 Ibid., p. 147.
30 Ibid., p. 148.

Chapter Five
33 Tullidge, *The Women of Mormondom*, p. 292.
33 Ibid., p. 294.
34 Snow, *Biography and Family Record*, p. 45.
34 Morgan, *Eliza R. Snow, An Immortal*, p. 11.
35 Eliza R. Snow, *Diary and Notebook* (sometimes called Nauvoo Journal), photocopy of holograph, L.D.S. Church Archives, Salt Lake City, Utah, August 22, 1842.
36 Mary Belnap Lowe, Statement, Ogden, Utah, May 12, 1941, L.D.S. Church Archives, Salt Lake City, Utah.
36 Snow, *Diary and Notebook*, June 29, 1842.
37 Snow, *Biography and Family Record*, p. 68.
37 *Woman's Exponent*, Salt Lake City, Utah, August 1, 1886.
37 Snow, *Diary and Notebook*, June 29, 1842.
38 Tullidge, *Women of Mormondom*, p. 295.
38 Ibid.
38 Ibid.
38 Ibid.
39 Snow, *Diary and Notebook*, September 23, 1842.
39 Tullidge, *Women of Mormondom*, p. 294.
40 Snow, *Diary and Notebook*, August 14, 1842.
40 Donna Hill, *Joseph Smith: The First Mormon*. Garden City, New York: Doubleday & Company, Inc., 1977, p. 352.

153

to Sister Eliza Snow," photocopy of manuscript, L.D.S. Church Archives, Salt Lake City, Utah.

56 Maureen Ursenbach Beecher, "Eliza R. Snow," in Vicky Burgess-Olson's *Sister Saints*. Provo, Utah: Brigham Young University Press, 1978, p. 7.

56 Ibid., p. 6.

57 *Hymns, The Church of Jesus Christ of Latter-day Saints*. Salt Lake City, Utah: Deseret Book Company, 1979, p. 139.

57 Joseph F. Smith, "Discourses," *Deseret Evening News*, February 9, 1895. This discourse was delivered January 20, 1895.

57 Wilford Woodruff, "Discourse," *The Latter-day Saints' Millenial Star*, 56 (April 9, 1894): 229. The discourse was delivered October 8, 1893.

58 Ellen Wallace, "Eliza Roxcy Snow Smith," *Young Women's Journal*, 21:8-13, January, 1910.

58 Letter from David McKay to Mrs. James Hood.

59 Orson F. Whitney, *History of Utah*. Salt Lake City, Utah, vol. IV, p. 573.

59 *The Western Galaxy*, March, 1888, p. 142.

Chapter Eight

61 Snow, *Biography and Family Record*, p. 70.

61 Ibid., p. 71.

62 Snow, *Diary and Notebook*, December 31, 1843.

62 Snow, *Biography and Family Record*, p. 72.

62 Andrew Jenson, *Latter-Day* [sic] *Saint Biographical Encyclopedia*, Salt Lake City, Utah: Andrew Jenson History Company, 1801, vol. III, p. 676.

64 Morgan, *Eliza R. Snow, An Immortal*, p. 13.

66 Snow, *Biography and Family Record*, pp. 80-82.

67 Morgan, *Eliza R. Snow, An Immortal*, pp. 234, 235.

68 Ibid.

68 Aurelia Spencer Rogers, *Life Sketches of Orson Spencer and Others, and History of Primary Work*. Salt Lake City, Utah: George Q. Cannon and Sons Co., 1898, p. 245.

Chapter Nine

72 Eliza R. Snow, *Pioneer Diary*, February 12, 1846—August 16, 1849, microfilm of holograph, L.D.S. Church Archives,

Page

Chapter Eleven

91 Tullidge, *Women of Mormondom*, p. 351.

92 Ibid.

92 Ibid.

92 Ibid.

93 Snow, *Pioneer Diary*, October 11, 1847.

93 Tullidge, *Women of Mormondom*, p. 352.

94 Brigham Young, Deed of Consecration, L.D.S. Church Archives, Salt Lake City, Utah, April 11, 1855, Book A, p. 249.

95 Snow, *Biography and Family Record*, p. 260.

97 Lion House Guide Service, mimeographed information used by tour guides at Brigham Young's Lion House, Salt Lake City, Utah.

98 Clarissa Young Spencer with Mabel Harmer, *Brigham Young At Home*. Salt Lake City, Utah: Deseret Book Company, 1940, p. 82.

99 Ibid., p. 33.

99 Ibid., p. 82.

Chapter Twelve

104 Snow, *Biography and Family Record*, p. 96.

104 Ibid.

106 Ibid.

107 *Utah Historical Quarterly*, Salt Lake City, Utah, vol. 43, no. 1, Winter, 1975.

108 Snow, *Biography and Family Record*, pp. 251-252.

108 Hannah Tapfield King, *Journal*, October 8, 1856, typescript, L.D.S. Church Archives, Salt Lake City, Utah.

109 Minutes, Tenth Ward Young Ladies Retrenchment Association, January 8, 1875, printed in *Woman's Exponent*, Salt Lake City, Utah, February 1, 1875.

109 Eliza R. Snow, "Simplicity," *Woman's Exponent*, June 1, 1877. Compare with Doctrine and Covenants 92:36.

109 Maureen Ursenbach Beecher in *Utah Historical Quarterly*, volume 43, no. 1, Winter, 1975, p. 40.

Chapter Thirteen

112 *Woman's Exponent*.

113 Relief Society of the Church of Jesus Christ of Latter-day

Saints.

Saints, *History of Relief Society 1842-1966.* Salt Lake City, Utah: General Board of Relief Society, 1966, p. 34.

114 Morgan, *Eliza R. Snow, An Immortal,* p. 579.

114 Ibid.

114 Ibid.

114 *Deseret News,* Salt Lake City, Utah, April 22, 1868.

115 *Woman's Exponent,* vol. 5, no. 4, July 15, 1876, p. 28.

115 Clarissa Young Spencer, *One Who Was Valiant.* Caldwell, Idaho: Caxton Printers, Ltd., 1940, p. 76.

115 Letter, Eliza R. Snow to Brigham Young, February 10, 1877, Brigham Young Collection, L.D.S. Church Archives, Salt Lake City, Utah.

117 Burgess-Olson, *Sister Saints,* p. 442.

118 Spencer, *Brigham Young At Home,* p. 84.

118 Ibid., p. 85.

118 Ibid.

119 Ibid., p. 86.

119 Morgan, *Eliza R. Snow, An Immortal,* p. 452.

120 "A Welcome," *Woman's Exponent,* vol. 9, April 1, 1881, p. 165.

Chapter Fourteen

122 Snow, *Biography and Family Record,* pp. 496, 497.

123 *Correspondence of Palestine Tourists; Comprising A Series of Letters By George A. Smith, Lorenzo Snow, Paul A. Schettler, and Eliza R. Snow, of Utah. Mostly written while traveling in Europe, Asia and Africa. In the years 1872 and 1873.* Salt Lake City, Utah: Deseret News Steam Printing Establishment, 1875, p. 4.

123 Ibid.

123 Ibid., p. 9.

123 Ibid., p. 12.

124 Ibid., p. 60.

124 "Pen Sketch of an Illustrious Woman," *Woman's Exponent,* July 1881, p. 187.

125 Snow, *Biography and Family Record,* p. 532.

125 Ibid.

125 Ibid., p. 533.

126 Ibid., p. 535.

126 Ibid., p. 542.

126 *Palestine Tourists,* p. 136.

127 Ibid., p. 137.

127 Ibid., p. 260.

127 Ibid.

128 Snow, *Biography and Family Record*, pp. 555-556.

129 Ibid., p. 561.

130 *Woman's Exponent*, June 15, 1881.

131 Snow, *Biography and Family Record*, p. 580.

131 Ibid.

131 *Woman's Exponent*, July 1, 1881.

132 Ibid., August 1, 1881.

Chapter Fifteen

136 *Pearl of Great Price*, Moses 4:22.

137 Jill C. Mulvay [Derr], "Eliza R. Snow and The Woman Question," *B.Y.U. Studies*, Winter, 1976, p. 251.

138 *Woman's Exponent*, September 1, 1875.

139 Ibid., September 15, 1875.

139 Ibid., April 1, 1876.

140 Tullidge, *Women of Mormondom*, p. 181.

140 Bruce R. McConkie, *Mormon Doctrine*. Salt Lake City, Utah: Bookcraft, 1966, p. 18.

140 *Woman's Exponent*, May 1, 1891.

141 Suza Young Gates with Leah D. Widstoe, *The Life Story of Brigham Young*. New York: The Macmillan Company, 1931, p. 361.

141 *Woman's Exponent*, September 15, 1884.

142 *The Improvement Era*, Salt Lake City, Utah, December 1919, vol. 23, p. 121.

142 Ibid.

142 Gates, *The Life Story of Brigham Young*, p. 361.

143 *Woman's Exponent*.

Chapter Sixteen

146 Morgan, *Eliza R. Snow, An Immortal*, p. 194.

146 From the Mary E. Rollins Lightner Papers, Brigham Young University Library, Provo, Utah.

146 Ibid.

146 Ibid.

147 *The Life and Labors of Eliza R. Snow Smith*. Salt Lake City, Utah: Juvenile Instructor Office, 1888, pp. 5, 6.

Page

147 Ibid., p. 6.

147 Ibid.

148 *The Life and Labors*, pp. 15-36.

148 *The Latter-day Saints' Millenial Star*, vol. 50, no. 1, January 2, 1888.

149 *The Life and Labors*, p. 37.

149 *Hymns, The Church of Jesus Christ of Latter-day Saints*, pp. 68, 139, 230, 285.

Bibliography

Barrett, Ivan J. *Heroines of the Church*. Leadership Week materials. Provo, Utah: Brigham Young University, 1973.

The Book of Mormon. Salt Lake City, Utah: The Church of Jesus Christ of Latter-day Saints, 1920 edition.

Burgess-Olson, Vicky. *Sister Saints*. Provo, Utah: Brigham Young University Press, 1978.

Bushman, Claudia L. *Mormon Sisters*. Salt Lake City, Utah: Olympus Publishing Co., 1976.

Deseret News. Salt Lake City, Utah, April 22, 1868.

Gates, Suza Young with Widstoe, Leah D. *The Life Story of Brigham Young*. New York: The Macmillan Company, 1931.

Hill, Donna. *Joseph Smith: The First Mormon*. Garden City, New York: Doubleday & Company, 1977.

The Holy Bible (King James version). Salt Lake City, Utah: Deseret Book Company.

Hymns, The Church of Jesus Christ of Latter-day Saints. Salt Lake City, Utah: Deseret Book Company, 1979.

The Improvement Era. Salt Lake City, Utah, July, 1973.

King, Hannah Tapfield. "Lines, Affectionately Addressed to

Sister Eliza Snow." Photocopy of manuscript, L.D.S. Church Archives, Salt Lake City, Utah.

King, Hannah Tapfield. *Journal*, October 8, 1856. Typescript, L.D.S. Church Archives, Salt Lake City, Utah.

Letter from David McKay to Mrs. James Hood, March 16, 1916. Typescript of holograph, L.D.S. Church Archives, Salt Lake City, Utah.

Letters from Emmeline B. Wells to Mary E. Rollins Lightner, February 10, 1887 and March 12, 1887. Mary E. Rollins Lightner papers, Brigham Young University Library, Provo, Utah.

Letter from Emily P. Young, April 28, 1886. Mary E. Rollins Lightner papers, Brigham Young University Library, Provo, Utah.

The Life and Labors of Eliza R. Snow Smith. Salt Lake City, Utah: Juvenile Instructor Office, 1888.

Lion House Guide Service. Mimeographed information used by tour guides at Brigham Young's Lion House. Salt Lake City, Utah.

Lowe, Mary Belnap. Statement made May 12, 1941, Ogden, Utah. Typescript of holograph, L.D.S. Church Archives, Salt Lake City, Utah.

Morgan, Nicholas G. *Eliza R. Snow, An Immortal: Selected Writings of Eliza R. Snow.* Salt Lake City, Utah: Nicholas G. Morgan Sr. Foundation, 1957.

McConkie, Bruce R. *Mormon Doctrine.* Salt Lake City, Utah: Bookcraft, 1966.

Mulvay [Derr], Jill C. "Eliza R. Snow and The Woman Question." *BYU Studies*, Winter, 1976.

Pearson, Carol Lynn. *Daughters of Light.* Provo, Utah: Trilogy Arts, 1973.

The Relief Society General Board Association. *History of Relief Society, 1842-1966.* Salt Lake City, Utah: The General Board of Relief Society, 1966.

Rogers, Aurelia Spencer, *Life Sketches of Orson Spencer and Others, and History of Primary Work.* Salt Lake City, Utah: George Q. Cannon and Sons Co., 1898.

Smith, Joseph F. "Discourses." *Deseret Evening News.* Salt Lake City, Utah, February 9, 1895.

Snow, Eliza R. *Biography and Family Record of Lorenzo Snow.* Salt Lake City, Utah: Deseret News Company, 1884.

Snow, Eliza R. *Diary and Notebook.* (Sometimes called Nauvoo Journal.) Photocopy of holograph, L.D.S. Church Archives, Salt Lake City, Utah, August 22, 1842.

Snow, Eliza R. *Pioneer Diary,* June 1, 1846-August 16, 1849. Microfilm of holograph, L.D.S. Church Archives, Salt Lake City, Utah.

Spencer, Clarissa Young with Harmer, Mabel. *Brigham Young At Home.* Salt Lake City, Utah: Deseret Book Company, 1940.

Spencer, Clarissa Young. *One Who Was Valiant.* Caldwell, Idaho: Caxton Printers, Ltd., 1940.

Tullidge, Edward W. *The Women of Mormondom.* New York: Tullidge and Crandall, 1877.

Utah Historical Quarterly, vol. 43, no. 1, Winter, 1975.

Wallace, Ellen. "Eliza Roxcy Snow Smith." *Young Women's Journal.* Salt Lake City, Utah, 21:8-13, January, 1910.

Western Courier. Ravenna, Ohio, February 14, 1829.

Whitney, Orson F. *History of Utah.* vol. IV. Salt Lake City, Utah.

Woman's Exponent. Salt Lake City, Utah, 1872-1914.

Woodruff, Wilford. "Discourse." *The Latter-day Saints' Millennial Star.* Salt Lake City, Utah, April 9, 1894.

Young, Brigham. Deed of Consecration. L.D.S. Church Archives. Salt Lake City, Utah, Book A, April 11, 1855.